Balhae,
The "Flourishing Kingdom of the East" As the Successor to Goguryeo

NAHF
History & Culture
Series

Balhae,
The "Flourishing Kingdom of the East" As the Successor to Goguryeo

Kim Eunkuk
Kwen Eunju
Kim Jinkwang

NORTHEAST ASIAN
HISTORY FOUNDATION

Publisher's Note

The countries of the East Asian region have historically shared close ties. Since ancient times, various ethnic groups have emerged on the Asian continent and formed nations. Conversely, wars of conquest have sometimes caused ethnic groups and nations to disappear. Countries such as Korea, China, and Japan have evolved from ancient times to the present day, developing through conflict and war on the one hand, and through exchange and cooperation on the other. As civilizations developed on the continent from the earliest times, they formed unique cultures through the exchange of materials and cultures. Modernity has been marked by conflicts between maritime and continental powers, as well as invasive imperialist wars. A particularly unfortunate period in history unfolded when Japan forcibly annexed Korea and invaded China.

Establishing a system of peace in East Asia requires overcoming the unfortunate history of the past and establishing a new paradigm of international relations. Unfortunately, however, unproductive nationalistic historical perspectives have tended to predominate in the early 21st century. When countries strongly emphasize a nationalistic viewpoint, distrust increases among neighboring nations, resulting in the regrettable situation of escalating conflicts and tensions.

The Northeast Asian History Foundation was established in 2006 with the aim of resolving conflicts arising from differences in historical perceptions in the East Asian region in order to promote cooperation and prosperity within a framework of peace. Over the years, the Foundation has conducted research on East Asian history and held international academic exchanges to bridge differences in historical perceptions. The results have been published in various series of historical publications and have received acclaim from many readers. However, most of these publications are in Korean, which has limited their ability to reach a global audience and facilitate cross-border communication with global citizens. Therefore, in order to share research results with the international community and create a platform for communication aiming to resolve differences in historical perceptions, the Foundation plans to publish the <History & Culture Series>.

The series will cover topics that can help people around the world understand issues that have caused disputes in East Asian history, encompassing territorial and maritime issues, among others. We hope that this series, published by the Northeast Asian History Foundation, can make a significant contribution to the accurate understanding of historical conflicts in the East Asian region and to bridging differences in historical perceptions.

Young-ho Lee
President of Northeast Asian History Foundation

Preface

This book, *Balhae, the "Flourishing Kingdom of the East" as the Successor to Goguryeo*, is part of the General Book Series published by the Northeast Asian History Foundation. This book aims to explain the history of the kingdom of Balhae (渤海, Ch. *Bohai;* J. *Bokkai,* 698-926) as it happened, in a language and format more accessible to the general readers, especially young people. It is hoped that this book will meet the need to make the history of Balhae more widely known to both domestic and foreign audiences.

In Korea, we sometimes hear the word Balhae in everyday life, as when a weather forecaster says, "Tomorrow, the high pressure that has developed in Balhae Bay will affect the Korean Peninsula." We know that Balhae in the Balhae Bay is the name of the kingdom that claimed to be the successor to Goguryeo after its fall. However, few people know that the original name of the Balhae kingdom at its founding was the Jinguk (震國 or 振國), not Balhae.

We also tend to think of Korean history as centered on the Korean Peninsula, but it should be noted that the geographical setting of Korean history has not always been limited to the Korean Peninsula, but extended beyond the Amnok River and the Duman River. Balhae played a crucial role as a transmitter of culture and goods in Northeast Asia, crossing across both rivers, and its territory included present-day North Korea and part of the Russian and Chinese territory. Moreover, Koreans consider Balhae as the counterpart of Silla to the south, and argue that Silla and Balhae together should be called the Southern and Northern Kingdoms (南北國). Thus, Balhae can be recognized as a bridge that connected Silla to the Northeast Asian continent to the north.

Balhae was very similar to Goguryeo (first century BCE - 668 CE). This is because the majority of those who founded Balhae were remnants from Goguryeo after its fall. Although the collapse of the state resulted in the end of the royal line, its people persevered. Balhae was founded in 698, only thirty years after the fall of Goguryeo. Balhae's founder, King Go (Dae Joyeong), paved the way for the restoration of old Goguryeo by incorporating the people of old Goguryeo and rebuilding the kingdom's fortresses, roads and more. Throughout the reign of 15 kings, Balhae solidified its position as the Haedongseongguk (海東盛國), the *"Flourishing Kingdom of the East"* which interacted not only with the Silla region to the south but also with Japan across the East Sea(Kr. Donghae 東海, Japan Sea). However, Balhae was destroyed by the Khitans in 926, resulting in a break in the royal succession. For the next 200 years, the descendants of the population of Balhae made active efforts to rebuild their kingdom, but they were unable to do so. Consequently, Korean history thereafter remained confined to the Korean Peninsula. Balhae can be considered the last kingdom in Korean history to rule both the land and sea at the same time.

Balhae, the Haedongseongguk, was the successor to Goguryeo and a transmitter of East Asian culture. It was undoubtedly an important part of Korean history, constituting the Southern and Northern Kingdoms period together with Silla. In this book, we have explored the reasons behind the claim that Balhae was the successor to Goguryeo and delved into the role of Balhae, the Flourishing Kingdom of the East, as a transmitter of East Asian culture.

This book consists of eight chapters. Chapter 1 serves as an introduction to the book. By examining how the history of Balhae has been perceived to date, we explore why the history of Balhae warrants attention. Chapter 2 tells the story of the founding of Balhae and highlights the achievements of King Go in raising Balhae's international stature. Chapter 3 reconstructs the foundation of the Balhae state, which was solidified during the reigns of the second king, King Mu, and the third king, King Mun. Chapter 4, which focuses on the tenth king, King Seon, depicts scenes of Balhae establishing itself as a center of East Asian culture. Chapter 5 examines Balhae's crisscrossing transportation routes and trade activities with neighboring states. Chapter 6 presents archaeological findings of Balhae's everyday culture, such as its pastimes, food, clothing, and residential structure characterized by ondol (hypocaust heating system). Chapter 7 reexamines the events related to the fall of Balhae. Additionally, it reviews the efforts of Balhae refugees to rebuild Balhae. In the final chapter, Chapter 8, we aim to continue the thread of thinking about how to perceive Balhae in order to integrate Balhae into the broader narrative of Korean history.

As I write this preface, I hope that readers will share the images of Balhae that this book tries to present. It is imperative to continue the task of recovering the history and culture of Balhae through historical and archaeological materials, and finding the meaning of Balhae for us in the present. It is my sincere hope that this book can serve as a friendly guide to understanding the history and culture of Balhae. I especially hope that it can serve as a stepping stone for young people, who will play a leading role in history, to understand Korean history.

Kim Eunkuk, representing the authorship

Contents

Publisher's Note ▪ 4
Preface ▪ 6

Chapter 1 **NARRATING BALHAE**
1. Attention to the History of Balhae ▪ 14
2. Balhae's Succession to Goguryeo as Told by
   Its Neighbors ▪ 20

Chapter 2 **REFOUNDING THE KINGDOM**
3. King Go as the Resettlement Facilitator
   for the Goguryeo Diaspora ▪ 30
4. Controversy Over the Initial Name of the Kingdom, Jinguk vs. Malgal ▪ 37

Chapter 3 **TERRITORIAL EXPANSION**
5. Territorial Domain of the Haedongseongguk ▪ 50
6. The Imperial Status of Balhae, as Established by King Mun ▪ 58
7. Reasons for Balhae's Sea Campaign against the Tang at Dengzhou ▪ 65
8. Japan's Plan to Subjugate Silla ▪ 73
9. Reasons for Moving the Capital Four Times ▪ 79

Chapter 4 **ESTABLISHING AUTHORITY**
10. Emergence of Suryeong and Territorial Expansion ▪ 92
11. King Seon: Enhancing Balhae's Stature as the Haedongseongguk ▪ 99
12. Universality and Specificity of Balhae's Culture ▪ 106

Chapter 5 **FOREIGN RELATIONSHIPS**
13. Exchanges with Neighboring Countries through Land and Sea · 116
14. Popularity of Balhae Products in East Asia · 123
15. Relations with Japan, as Described in Diplomatic Documents · 129

Chapter 6 **PEOPLE'S LIFE**
16. Tombs of Princess Jeonghye and Jeonghyo · 140
17. Three Balhae Men Are a Match for a Tiger · 147
18. Pastime · 155
19. Clothing Styles and Textiles · 160
20. Letters and Literary Culture · 169
21. Housing with Ondol · 177

Chapter 7 **LOST THE KINGDOM**
22. Collapsed Due to Eruption of Mount Baekdu? · 188
23. Fierce Battle over Liaodong and the Fall of Balhae · 198
24. Revivalism of Balhae Refugees · 204
25. Perceptions of the Goryeo Ruling Class toward Balhae · 212
26. Seven Generations of the Balhae Jang Clan · 218

Chapter 8 **LOSING THE HISTORY?**
27. How Can Balhae's Legacies Be Inherited? · 228

Bibliography · 237
Index · 244

Note:

1. This book is a translation of 『해동성국, 고구려를 품은 발해』 (Northeast Asian History Foundation, 2019).
2. In this book, personal names, place names, and official names are rendered in the modern pronunciations of Korean, Chinese, and Japanese.
3. Romanization of Korean pronunciation follows the National Institute of Korean Language's notation, not the McKeon-Reishauer system.

CHAPTER 1
NARRATING BALHAE

1.
Attention to the History of Balhae

Kim Eunkuk

Balhae and East Asia

Research on the history of Balhae (Ch. Bohai, 渤海), like other topics in Korean history, has made outstanding progress since the twentieth century. The history of Balhae has long been an important international research area, as not only scholars from the two Koreas, but also from China, Japan, and Russia have produced research results that are essential references.

The international scope of research on the history of Balhae means that it is no longer possible to confine this topic to the framework of Korean history, making it necessary to incorporate the research products of other countries as references in one's own research. This has contributed to the diversification of views and opinions on Balhae, but that diversification also depends strongly on which historical sources researchers choose to focus on and how they interpret those sources. Therefore, it is important to understand the textual sources and interpretive frameworks that are used when researching Balhae's history.

Another problem in researching the history of Balhae is the lack of textual sources. Long ago, Yu Deukgong (柳得恭), a Joseon scholar of Practical Learning (實學) tried to reconstruct the history of Balhae based on textual sources, but this attempt simply led to an awareness of the limitations of textual sources. Fortunately, however, the lack of textual sources can be overcome by the archaeological discoveries of Balhae-related remains and artifacts, as well as the field research at Balhae-related sites that has been a topic of major interest in recent years. Moreover, thanks to the normalization of diplomatic relations with Russia and China in the 1990s, South Korean scholars have taken part in these new trends in the study of Balhae history and have personally surveyed and investigated the historical sites scattered throughout Manchuria, which are thought to be related to Korean history.

Field research on Balhae's historical remains has opened a new dimension in approaching Balhae's history beyond conventional research methodologies. It is very encouraging that several field research reports on the Balhae-related historical sites have been published in recent years. South Korean scholars have also begun to participate in such field research, following in the footsteps of Chinese and North Korean scholars in the 1960s. This participation is a milestone in the research on the history of Balhae.

However, despite the development of more diverse methods for researching Balhae's history, tit is regrettable that research on Balhae in South Korea has been largely limited to textual sources. This is because almost all the remains of Balhae are located in the current territories of China, Russia, and North Korea. Consequently, research on Balhae has been conducted not only in Korea, but also in China, Russia, and Japan, making the emergence of local perspectives inevitable.

These local perspectives have naturally led to nationalistic interpretations of historical sources relevant to Balhae. Chinese scholars have taken a Chinese imperial (i.e., Tang) approach to the history of Balhae, while Japanese scholars have tended to view it through the framework of Japan-Balhae relations. Meanwhile, many Korean scholars have argued that Balhae and Silla together should be identified as the Southern and Northern Kingdoms (南北國), thus incorporating Balhae into Korean history.

Chinese scholars have long considered Balhae to be a "local feudal regime of the Tang period," and the term "Bohai of the Tang" is currently placed on the signboard at the sites of Balhae's Capital Sanggyeong Yongcheon-bu (上京 龍泉府), thus representing a viewpoint where Balhae is considered to be part of Tang history. Since the launch of China's Northeast Project (東北工程), Korean scholars have been critically analyzing and examining this project.

Under these circumstances, it is no longer valid to use the lack of historical sources as a reason for the lack of in-depth research on the history of Balhae in comparison with other areas of Korean history. The absence of historical sources today does not necessarily mean that they were absent from the beginning. After all, they disappeared over the course of time under the special circumstances of certain periods.

Starting the Book, *Balhae*, the "Flourishing Kingdom of the East" as the Successor to Goguryeo

This book is part of a series of books published by the Northeast Asian History Foundation for the general public. As mentioned above, research into the history of Balhae has been hampered by disputes and differing interpretations. How to write a history that can be read by the general public is not an easy question to answer. Selecting the topics to be covered and forming the overall framework of the book proved to be as difficult as writing it. In the course of this work, the title of the book, *Balhae, the "Flourishing Kingdom of the East" As the Successor to Goguryeo*, was finally conceived. With this as our motto, the authors have been able to paint a broad picture of the history of Balhae as a state that inherited the legacies of Goguryeo and formed the Southern and Northern Kingdoms together with Silla.

Since this book was originally written in Korean for Korean readers, the authors have tried to present the Korean perspective to readers. At the same time, however, in light of the many controversial aspects of research on the history of Balhae, they have also tried to be descriptive in narrating the historical events of Balhae. Kim Eunkuk (an honorary researcher fellow of the Northeast Asian History Foundation) is the main author of the book. Three co-authors, including Kim Eunkuk again, Kwen Eunju (a chief researcher fellow of the Northeast Asian History Foundation), and Kim Jinkwang (a chief researcher of the Academy of Korean Studies), contributed to the 27 topics covering the history of Balhae from its founding to its decline and aftermath. Thanks to their dedicated efforts to produce a readable and public-friendly book through a series of discussions and seminars, the book has finally been published.

After the prologue, the main themes of the book are presented as follows.

- The history of Balhae from a Korean perspective rather than that of neighboring nations, focusing on the founder King Go's (高王) perceptions of the identity and stature of his new kingdom
- The efforts of King Mu (武王) and King Mun (文王) to lay the foundations of the Haedongseongguk (海東盛國, *Flourishing Kingdom of the East*)

- King Seon's (宣王) historical and cultural achievements, which greatly enhanced Balhae's international reputation
- Balhae's dynamic foreign relations with neighboring countries
- Balhae's everyday life and material culture
- Understanding and significance of Balhae's decline, which ended in 926 when its last king succumbed to the Khitans (契丹) invaders

We hope that this book will provide an opportunity to reassess and acknowledge the history of Balhae, many aspects of which have often been misunderstood due to the lack of written and archaeological sources.

2.
Balhae's Succession to Goguryeo as Told by Its Neighbors

Kim Jinkwang

A Historical Debate Triggered by China's Northeast Project

In the late 1990s, South Korean scholars were shocked by the news of China's national project to develop its northeastern provinces. While the purpose of the project, on the surface, was the economic revitalization of China's northeastern region, concerns about the distortion of historical issues that might arise after the collapse of North Korea intensified. As Korean scholars had experienced academic clashes with their Chinese counterparts during China's attempt to include the ancient Goguryeo murals on the territory of present-day China on the UNESCO World Heritage List, their concerns about the Chinese move were all the more serious. It was known that Chinese scholars and authorities were trying to incorporate Goguryeo history into Chinese history, even though Goguryeo had long been recognized as part of Korean history. The *Samguk sagi* (三國史記, History of the Three Kingdoms), Korea's oldest surviving history book, treated Goguryeo as a legitimate member of the Korean Three Kingdoms, but Chinese dynastic histories treated it as a border state outside the Chinese empire.

In addition to Goguryeo, Balhae has also become a target of China's nationalization of its history. The lack of records makes it difficult to know what really happened, and even the records that do exist are mostly written from a Chinese perspective. Whenever new aspects of Balhae's history have been revealed, a subjective interpretation reflecting China's national-centered historical perspective has been repeated. Unfortunately, the discussion about the attribution of Balhae's history continues to run in parallel.

Gap in Historical Understanding

The two official histories of the Tang dynasty, the *Jiu Tangshu* (舊唐書, Old Book of Tang) and the *Xin Tangshu* (新唐書, New Book of Tang), tell the story of the founding of Balhae. The *Jiu Tangshu* is a history of the Tang compiled in 945 in the midst of the chaotic period of the Five Dynasties and Ten States (907-960), only twenty years after the fall of Balhae. The *Xin Tangshu* is a history of the Tang compiled in 1060 in the Song era, some 140 years after the fall of Balhae. The former, though less refined in style, captures the appearance of

Balhae during that era as it was, while the latter, more refined and elegant in words and expressions, contains aspects that were not included in the former. It should be noted that although both books are accounts of Tang history, they differ in their portrayal of historical events. The reliability of the materials can vary depending on the time of compilation, just as inscriptions on metal and stone, which contain the contents of that time, and historical records, which reflect later historical perspectives, show differences in reliability.

The historical origin of Balhae has been linked to the origin of its founder King Go, Dae Joyeong (大祚榮). The *Jiu Tangshu* states that Dae Joyeong "originally belonged to a branch (Kr. byeoljong, Ch. biezhong; 別種) of the Goguryeo people," while the *Xin Tangshu* describes him as "belonging to the Songmal Malgal (Ch. Sumo Mohe, 粟末靺鞨) associated with Goguryeo." The shift in describing the identity of Dae Joyeong from the Goguryeo branch to the Songmal Malgal seems to reflect the changing view of Song Chinese historians about Balhae based on the Neo-Confucian theory of legitimate succession (Ch. Zhengtong, 正統). Song Chinese historians supported the Malgal (Ch. Mohe) as the legitimate successor to their supposed ancestors, the Suksin (Ch. Sushen, 肅愼), the Eumnu (Ch. Yilu, 挹婁), and the Mulgil (Ch. Wuji, 勿吉), who they believed had historically dominated the northeastern border region of China. On the other hand, Goryeo (高麗, then the second unified kingdom in Korea) seriously challenged the legitimacy of the Khitan Liao who had destroyed Balhae by continuously accepting Balhae refugees and abandoning the Liao's present camels at the Manbu Bridge (萬夫橋) in an attempt to undermine diplomatic relations with them.

Balhae as Perceived by Its Neighboring Countries

The recognition that Balhae succeeded Goguryeo as a separate entity from the Tang can be found in several historical sources. The historical accounts that help us recognize Balhae's identity are as follows: "An envoy was sent to the northern land (i.e., Balhae) [from Silla]" in the *Samguk sagi*; "A former general of Goguryeo founded the kingdom" in the *Samguk yusa* (三國遺事, Memories of the Three Kingdoms); "The remnants of Goguryeo gathered around Mt. Taebaek to establish the Kingdom" in Choi Chiwon's (崔致遠) *Memorial to Thank [the Tang Emperor] for Not Allowing the Northern State (i.e., Balhae envoys) to Sit Higher Than [Silla envoys]* (謝不許北國居上表); "land of relatives" to refer to Balhae in the *Goryeosa* (高麗史, History of Goryeo). Balhae subjects were also eligible to take civil service examinations under the Tang Bingongke (賓貢科) examination track designed for foreign candidates, illustrating that Balhae remained a separate political entity from the Tang. This view of Balhae as an independent state was carried over to some of the late Joseon scholars of Practical Learning such as Yu Deukgong, who wrote the *Balhaego* (渤海考, *Study of Balhae*) and attempted to incorporate Balhae history into Korean history.

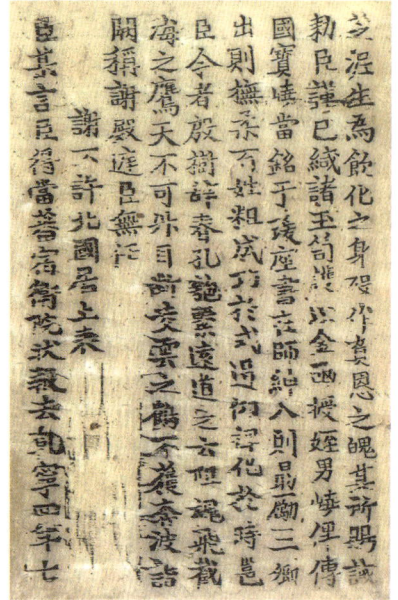

Choi Chiwon (崔致遠)
Memorial to Thank [the Tang emperor] for Not Allowing the Northern State (i.e., Balhae Envoys) to Sit Higher than [Silla Envoys] (謝不許北國居上表)

They introduced the concept of "Southern and Northern Kingdoms" and sharply criticized the ruling elite of Goryeo for not compiling its history while making efforts to accept Balhae refugees.

Balhae considered itself an independent state in its diplomatic relations with the Tang, the Turks, Silla, and Japan. In a diplomatic letter first sent to Japan in 727, Balhae's King Mu claimed that Balhae had "recovered the old land of Goguryeo and regained the old customs of Buyeo (扶餘)," making it clear to the outside world that his kingdom had inherited not only the territory of Goguryeo but also the cultural legacies of the preceding Buyeo kingdom. In sharp contrast to the Chinese description of Balhae as having been founded by a leader of the Songmal Malgal people, the founding kings of Balhae themselves proclaimed its distinctive identity as the successor of Goguryeo in the international arena. Moreover, King Mun referred to himself as the "Grandson of Heaven (天孫)", embracing the notion of independent origin (出自) as seen in the precedents of Buyeo's King Dongmyeong, Goguryeo's Jumong, and the stele inscription of Great King Gwanggaeto (廣開土大王碑文). He also proclaimed his belief in Balhae as the successor to Goguryeo by referring to its name as *Goryeo* instead of Balhae, and by calling himself King of Goryeo instead of King of Balhae.

The golden crown recently discovered in the M13 tomb of the Mt. Longtou tomb complex in present-day Helong City, Jilin-sheng, has three pieces of highly elaborate and detailed leaf-shaped decorations. It evokes the image of Goguryeo bird-feather headgear, and is considered to be a Goguryeo model. Bird-feather headgear is found in many records and paintings, and the image of a person wearing it can also be found on silver chests that were given to foreigners as gifts. In addition, the tomb inscription discovered in Princess Jeonghye's tomb tells that the Balhae court adopted the Goguryeo custom of observing a three-year mourning period. The structure of the tomb also features horizontal shafts leading to stone burial chambers and composite ceilings, reflecting the succession from the Goguryeo model. In addition, excavated Balhae dwellings have remains of ondol, a common heating device used by Goguryeo people. All of these pieces of evidence confirm the statement that Balhae "recovered the old land of Goguryeo and regained the old customs of Buyeo."

"A Nation That Forgets Its History Has No Future"

Due to the lack of records, it is not easy to grasp the reality. However, there is no doubt that Balhae is a part of Korean history, because it is clear from various literary and archaeological sources that there was a time when the unified Silla in the south coexisted with Balhae in the north, which was the heir to Goguryeo.

In his *Balhaego*, Yu Deukgong, who first introduced the concept of the "Southern and Northern Kingdoms" in Korean history, sharply criticized that "the reason why Goryeo was unable to expand its power was because it failed to compile the history of Balhae despite its efforts to take in its refugees." It should be noted that he did not simply point out the error of not compiling the history of Balhae, but criticized the ruling elite of Goryeo for not cultivating an appropriate historical consciousness about Balhae, even though they recognized Balhae as the "land of our relatives" and rejected diplomatic relations with the Khitans, who destroyed Balhae, by abandoning the Khitan present camels at the Manbu Bridge.

A nation that forgets its history has no future. It should be remembered that the history of Balhae is a part of Korean history, and the more than two hundred years that Balhae and Silla coexisted constitute the Southern and Northern Kingdoms period in Korean history. The exodus of refugees from Balhae after its fall continued for a century until the era of the eighth king of Goryeo, Hyeonjong. While the remains and relics of Balhae have remained in present-day China and Russia, an immeasurable cultural and spiritual heritage has been passed down to modern Koreans through the historical line of succession from Goryeo to Joseon.

CHAPTER 2
REFOUNDING THE KINGDOM

3.
King Go as the Resettlement Facilitator for the Goguryeo Diaspora

Kim Eunkuk

Balhae as Living History in East Asia

The history of Balhae cannot be viewed as part of the history of any one country, as most of the territory of Balhae spans the present-day three northeastern provinces of China, part of the Yeonhaeju, and North Korea. Naturally, nation-state perceptions strongly influence how each state perceives Balhae's history, resulting in significant differences. At some point, Balhae has already become a subject in the international academic field of East Asia.

In 1998, researchers from North and South Korea, China, Russia, Japan, and other countries celebrated the 1,300th anniversary of the founding of Balhae with various events. These included international academic conferences, attempts to explore Balhae's sea routes, and the publication of various books and translation works. In Russia, a

The Commemorative Special Stamp Set Dedicated to Dae Joyeong, Issued by Korea Post on November 17, 2011.

ginseng wine was even released to celebrate the 1300th anniversary of Balhae. In South Korea, a raft named *Balhae 1300* was launched as part of an attempt to explore the Balhae sea route, but unfortunately it was unsuccessful. These efforts, as depicted in the song *Dreaming of Balhae* by Seo Taiji and Boys, symbolize the recognition of the ancient Southern and Northern Kingdoms in the modern era of divided Korea.

In 2006-2007, the historical drama *Dae Joyeong* aired on KBS, sparking a K-drama craze among audiences throughout East Asia. In 2008, the Northeast Asian History Foundation organized an interna-

Dae Joyeong DDH 997

tional conference to bring together scholars from around the world interested in researching the history and culture of Balhae.

Since then, interest in Dae Joyeong (the founder of Balhae) has continued to grow. On November 17, 2011, Korea Post released a special commemorative stamp set dedicated to Dae Joyeong. The theme of the issue was *Reviving the Story of the Founding of Balhae through Stamps*. The interest in Dae Joyeong has led to a product, marking another step in restoring Balhae's status as a state. Through four themes related to the founding of Balhae, the stamps symbolically represent how Balhae once possessed the largest territory in our history, inherited and embraced the cultures of the Goguryeo and Tang dynasties, and evolved into the great eastern kingdom, known as the Haedongseongguk (海東盛國, *Flourishing Kingdom of the East*).

Balhae was a maritime and continental power, which controlled both land and sea. Through the East Sea, diplomatic missions frequently traveled to and from Japan. In the West Sea, naval battles and trade with the Tang dynasty showcased Balhae's advanced navigational and shipbuilding skills. In modern times, the name Dae Joyeong proudly adorns a South Korean naval vessel that has gained fame for its involvement in anti-piracy operations in the waters of Somalia.

King Go and the Stature of Balhae

Let's return to the northeastern region of China, which became the stage for Balhae's history. Mt. Dongmo (東牟山), where Dae Joyeong proclaimed the revival of Goguryeo, may not be particularly big or high, but even now, if you climb up there, you can see the fortress walls built along the ridges. This strategic stronghold took advantage of the natural terrain to provide a commanding view of the surrounding area at a glance. On the sunny slopes of Mt. Dongmo, there are tombs built by local people, and the impressive tombstones shine brightly in the sunlight. They exude a sacred aura, as if embodying the spirit of King Go, Dae Joyeong, who founded the Jinguk (i.e., Balhae).

China has recently been promoting projects to preserve historical sites and convert them into parks, and the ruins of Balhae are one of them. In particular, a statue of King Dae Joyeong of Balhae stands on the site of Sanggyeongseong (上京城), the former capital of Balhae. In

Portrait of King Go (Dae Joyeong) of Balhae

present-day Dunhua (敦化), the place where Balhae was founded and Mt. Dongmo is located, a visitor can see Balhae Square. However, the content and form of these sculptures clearly reflect China's perception of Balhae's history. China views Balhae as a regime established by local ethnic minorities during the Tang dynasty and classifies it as a vassal state of Tang. However, in order to establish a common understanding of Balhae's history in East Asia, it is important to recognize the authentic status of Balhae and use the title of *King Go* without imposing a Chinese perspective.

The historical drama *Dae Joyeong* depicts the remarkable achievements of young Dae Joyeong during the period before and after the fall of Goguryeo. He was born during the Battle of Ansi in 645, making him already over 50 years old when he proclaimed the revival of Goguryeo at Mt. Dongmo, and over 70 years old when he died in 719. His successful reconstruction of Goguryeo was due not only to his outstanding leadership and bravery, but also to the dedicated efforts of the Goguryeo refugees over the course of 30 years. After founding Balhae, he laid the foundation for an open nation that encouraged interactions with neighboring countries.

Now is the time to elevate the status of Dae Joyeong, the founder of Balhae, to the title of his respectful posthumous name, King Go (高王, King of Highness), befitting of the greatness of the once renowned maritime kingdom. The act of enshrining the standard portrait of King Go in 2012 is part of this effort. King Go was a symbolic figure to whom the Korean diaspora turned after the fall of Balhae. Upon further reflection, I would like to send a letter with a commemorative stamp of Dae Joyeong to the kingdom of Balhae that he ruled, as a way to send my greetings through the ages.

4.
Controversy Over the Initial Name of the Kingdom, Jinguk vs. Malgal

Kwen Eunju

The Chinese Argument for Defining the Initial Name of Balhae as *Malgal*

The early name of Balhae is given as Jinguk (震國 or 振國). However, there has been a long-standing debate within the Chinese academic community over the early name of Balhae, suggesting that the initial name was Malgal (Ch.Mohe, 靺鞨). This theory, known as the Malgal theory, states that the ruling ethnic group of Balhae was not Goguryeo but the Malgal people, leading to the claim that Malgal was the name of the nation. According to this theory, when Dae Joyeong first proclaimed himself king of Jinguk, he used it only as a title and never used the term as the name of the country.

The proponents of the Malgal theory make their argument on the basis of the following facts: the *Jiu Tangshu* (舊唐書, *Old Book of Tang*)

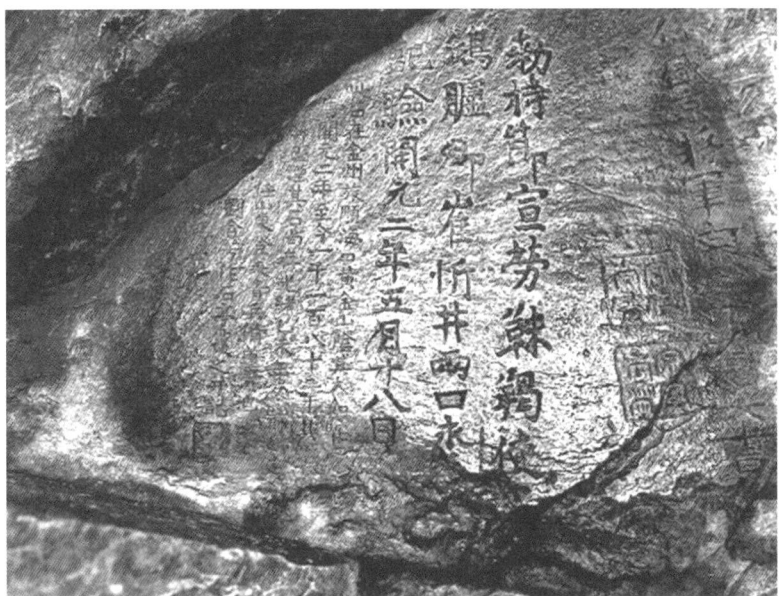

Malgal-sa (靺鞨使) on Cui Xin's Stone Inscription

did not refer to the Biography of Balhae as that of Balhae, but as that of Balhae Malgal (Ch. Bohai Mohe). They also refer to the Biography of Balhae in the *Xin Tangshu* (新唐書, *New Book of Tang*), in which Emperor Xuanzong of Tang used the name Balhae and discarded the term Malgal, only after appointing Dae Joyeong as king of Balhae. Moreover, the stone inscription left by Cui Xin (崔忻), an envoy sent to Balhae to appoint Dae Joyeong as king, refers to his official position as *Malgal-sa* (靺鞨使, Ch. Mohe-shi).

In fact, the theory that the early name of Balhae was *Malgal* was considered a minority view even in China. However, in the 2000s, this theory was expanded and reproduced without proper scrutiny, and became widely accepted as if it were an established fact after China's Northeast Project, leading to significant issues.

Why Did the Tang Dynasty Refer Balhae to Malgal or Balhae Malgal?

The primary records indicating that Balhae used Jinguk as its early name for the country can be seen as follows: The *Bohai Mohe chuan* (渤海靺鞨傳, Biography of Balhae Malgal) in the *Jiu Tangshu* says, "[Dae Joyeong] took the throne of the state of Jinguk," and the *Bohai chuan* (渤海傳, Biography of Balhae) of the *Xin Tangshu* mentions that "[Dae Joyeong] titled himself king of the state of Jinguk." In addition, Choi Chiwon of Silla wrote in the *Memorial to Thank [the Tang emperor] for Not Allowing the Northern State (i.e., Balhae Envoys) to Sit Higher Than [Silla envoys]* (謝不許北國居上表) that "at first [Balhae] called itself the state of Jinguk." This evidence supports the fact that Balhae used Jinguk as its country name in its early days.

However, the Chinese academic community argues for the Malgal theory because the Tang dynasty sometimes referred to Balhae as Malgal or Balhae Malgal. However, it is important to note that these were only alternative names used by the Tang, not the name that Balhae used for itself. It is inappropriate to claim that the name of a country is based solely on what others called it or any nicknames they used.

Then why did the Tang dynasty call Balhae *Malgal or Balhae Malgal*? First, the Tang dynasty had a difficult history with Goguryeo, and they did not want to recognize Balhae as the legitimate successor of Goguryeo. Second, from the Tang dynasty's perspective, Balhae was founded through a rebellion led by Dae Joyeong, Goguryeo refugees, and the Malgal people. As a result, the Tang dynasty intentionally avoided using the name Jinguk, which represented Balhae's independence.

In addition, the fact that Balhae was referred to Malgal or Balhae Malgal also reflected its early relationship with the surrounding Malgal groups. Firstly, Dae Joyeong was from the Songmal Malgal (Ch. Sumo Mohe) lineage, but he had become a figure who was recognized as "belonging to a branch of the Goguryeo people" or "a former general of Goguryeo." In other words, he was considered a person of Goguryeo descent and of the Malgal lineage. His dual identity played a crucial role in unifying not only Goguryeo refugees but also the various Malgal factions that had been under the direct or indirect control of Goguryeo during the establishment of Balhae.

Secondly, in the early stages of the establishment of Balhae, the Malgal groups that were integrated into or allied with Jinguk were those with close ties to Goguryeo, called *Goguryeo Malgals*. These people later became known as Balhae Malgals. In 713, Cui Xin, the first envoy sent to Balhae by the Tang dynasty, was given the title *Malgal-sa* (靺鞨使) instead of Jinguksa with the intention of including these groups. After the visit of Cui Xin, the Malgal included in Balhae Malgal paid tribute to the Tang, and in 740, when Balhae assimilated these Malgals as Balhae's subjects, the term Balhae Malgal disappeared from use, providing evidence of this process.

In fact, the Tang dynasty's deliberate use of Malgal or Balhae Malgal to refer to Balhae was due to the complex situation in which Dae Joyeong was not only the king of Jinguk but also the king of Malgal. Therefore, Malgal was not the official name of Balhae in its early days; instead, it was an alternative name that partially reflected the circumstances of the time.

Possible Candidates for the First Name of Balhae

The reason why Balhae chose Jinguk as its early country name remains unclear, leaving us curious. When a new country establishes its name, it often references the name of the leading force in its establishment, a geographical name, or a historically related country name.

The establishment of Balhae was strongly influenced by the Goguryeo revival movement, and the groups involved in its founding, as well as the founding territory, had deep ties to Goguryeo. Therefore, when Balhae was founded in 698, it is highly probable that they considered names related to Goguryeo when choosing their initial country name.

The various Goguryeo-related names found in literature, inscriptions, and other written sources include country names, the names of people, geographical locations, directions, metaphors, and other expressions. Let's explore the possibility that Balhae considered these names as potential candidates for their initial country name.

Considering that Goryeo, founded by King Taejo, Wang Geon (太祖 王建), took its name from Goguryeo, and Joseon, founded by King Taejo, Yi Seonggye (太祖 李成桂), took its name from Gojoseon, the first names that come to mind for the original name of Balhae might be those directly related to Goguryeo. In reality, however, such names were not adopted. This decision might have been shaped by the political climate of the neighboring countries that bordered Goguryeo at the time. As a newly formed state, adopting the name of the once-powerful Goguryeo might have been viewed as posing a risk for diplomatic tensions with the neighboring countries. Furthermore, the direct descendants of Goguryeo's last king, King Bojang, lived in the Tang dynasty, and many Goguryeo people, including King Bojang's grandson, Anseung, resided in Silla. Under these circumstances, using the name Goguryeo could have caused diplomatic disputes, so it was probably not a viable option.

Other names were used to refer to Goguryeo, including Gojoseon (古朝鮮), Yodong (遼東), Dongyi (東夷), and Haedong (海東). However, these nicknames were essentially used by outsiders of Goguryeo, and reflected their perceptions rather than how Goguryeo saw itself.

For example, the term Gojoseon did not imply an acknowledgement of historical continuity or kinship with Goguryeo. Instead, it emphasized the Gija Joseon (箕子朝鮮) or Han-Sa-gun (漢四郡), which was within the framework of China's universal order, and reflected the Tang dynasty's intention to incorporate Goguryeo into its own order. Yodong and Haedong denoted the borders between China and Goguryeo, while Dongyi was a discriminatory term used within the Chinese-centered universal order to refer to eastern barbarians. Therefore, these nicknames could not be considered as potential initial names for Balhae, as they were associated with the perspectives of external parties rather than reflecting Balhae's self-perception.

What, then, is the origin of the name Jinguk? It is interesting to note that in the 7th century, even though there was no direct connection with Goguryeo, terms such as Samhan (三韓, Three Han), Jinhan (辰韓), Mahhan (馬韓), and Byeonhan (弁韓) were often used as nicknames for Goguryeo. Many scholars believe that Balhae's initial country name, Jinguk, was derived from the term Samhan or directly from Jinhan.

If Jinguk is indeed derived from Jinhan, the question arises as to why Goguryeo was called Samhan or Jinhan. There may be historical reasons that led to the selection of Jinguk as the initial name of Balhae. Recent research suggests that it may be related to Goguryeo's destruction of the Han (漢) Chinese Commanderies of Nangnang (Ch. Lolang, 樂浪) and Daebang (Ch. Daifang, 帶方), and its control over the

Jinhan (辰韓) in the Epitaph of Go Mo, a Goguryeo Remnant

region. After the fall of Gojoseon, the Chinese tried to extend control over the Han (韓, the southern power on the Korean Peninsula) through its two commanderies in northern Korea, Nangnang and Daebang. However, Goguryeo's southern expansion dealt a severe blow to Chinese rule when they lost control of the commanderies. Goguryeo expanded its territory and established its capital in Pyongyang, a center of Han control, thus creating an overlapping image of Goguryeo and the Han. Over time, the Han factions were recognized as Jinhan, and it is possible that Jinhan was used in parallel with Han (or Samhan), the broader term. This may be why Goguryeo, which occupied the region, was referred to as Jinhan.

The name of Balhae in early period, Jinguk, was most likely derived from the nickname Jinhan, which was used for Goguryeo. The likely connection between Jinguk and Jinhan can be inferred from their similar pronunciation. This probability is even higher when we consider that there are historical instances in which Balhae was called Jinhan. One such example can be found in the *Inscription of the Shrine Dedicated to Qian Liu, the King of the Wuyue Kingdom* (吳越王錢公生祠堂碑), where the term Jinhan can be seen.

於是, 南踰駱越, 北暨辰韓, 東極滄溟, 西臨黑水, 莫不來庭捧贄.

At that time, they crossed the Luoyue (駱越) in the south, reached Chenhan (Kr. Jinhan, 辰韓) in the north, extended to Cangmei (滄溟) in the east, and arrived at Heishu (黑水) in the west. In all directions, they came to the court of Wuyue State and paid tribute without exception.

This inscription was dedicated to a man named Qian Liu (錢鏐, 852-932). Qian Liu was the founder of the Wuyue Kingdom during the Five Dynasties period (Ch. Wudai, 五代) at the end of the Tang dynasty. In the first year of the Later Liang dynasty (後梁, 907) era, he proclaimed himself the king of the Wuyue and became the military commissioner of Huainan (淮南). This tombstone inscription predates the fall of the Later Liang, specifically belonging to a time before Qian Liu assumed the kingship of Wuyue in 923. Records in books such as the *Jiu Wudaishi* (舊五代史), the *Xin Wudaishi* (新五代史,) and the *Cefu*

Yuangui (冊府元龜) indicate that Balhae had active exchanges with Qian Liu's Wuyue, and it is documented that Balhae's envoys visited Wuyue annually from 907 to 912. During this close relationship, Balhae was the only country in the north that could be called Jinhan. The continued use of the nickname Jinhan until the end of Balhae may be linked to the historical use of Jinhan to refer to Goguryeo, as well as its association with Balhae's original name, Jinguk, which was derived from that term.

Implied Meaning of Jinguk as the First Name of Balhae

Why, then, did the initial name of Balhae, Jinguk, use the Chinese character 振 or 震, instead of 辰 as in Jinhan?

We do not know what the character Jin (辰) meant in Samhan, but it is clear that it is a Chinese character transliteration of Jinguk, which was the name given to the people of the ancient southern Korean Peninsula before the Three Kingdoms period. It is also unclear whether the character 辰 originally had the meaning of east. The interpretation of Chinese based on its characters' meaning was developed later, in the Three Kingdoms period at the earliest, and the character 辰 seems to have acquired the meaning of east with the development of foreign trade and the growth of the ancient states. The Chinese began to use words meaning east, such as *Haedong* (Ch. haidong, east of the sea), to refer to Manchuria and the Korean Peninsula, and ancient Koreans were also very conscious of being an eastern power as opposed to that of the west. Therefore, the meaning of east (東) could have been added to the name or nicknames of Korean states.

The characters 辰, 振, and 震 are all pronounced *jin* in Korean. Likewise, they are pronounced almost the same in modern Chinese (辰 [*chen*], 震[*zhen*], and 振[*zhen*]), and they were most probably pronounced similarly in the Tang times as well. Since the characters han (韓) and guk (國, kingdom) are interchangeable (i.e., they have the same meaning), the compound words Jinhan (辰韓), Jinguk (振國), and Jinguk (振國) are all transliterations of the same entity. The use of 振 or 震 instead of 辰, for the first name of Balhae should not be interpreted as reflecting a different origin of the name. As circumstances changed, new meanings may have been added to characters, leading to changes in the characters used.

The reason why Balhae chose Jinguk for its initial national name was probably because Jinhan (辰韓) was originally used as a nickname for Goguryeo. However, by the time Balhae was founded, the term had acquired the meaning of east. Thus, the name Jinguk implied that it was the eastern kingdom that succeeded Goguryeo. When written in characters, the choice of 振, which means "to rouse or to invigorate," suggests that Balhae was a newly established country determined to resist the influence of the Tang dynasty. Similarly, the name Silla (新羅) originated in Saro (斯盧), but as the country grew, it took on a political implication—namely, that "the king's influence is constantly renewed and embraces all directions."

In conclusion, the original name of Balhae was not Malgal but Jinguk. The name Jinguk derived from an alternative name for Goguryeo, and it may have reflected the hopes of Dae Joyeong and the founding group of Balhae to become a newly rising country of the east. Samhan (or Jinhan) was a longstanding alternative name for Korea from the 7th century through the Goryeo and Joseon dynasties. It is significant that Balhae shared this name.

CHAPTER 3
TERRITORIAL EXPANSION

5.
Territorial Domain of the Haedongseongguk

Kim Jinkwang

Another Kingdom to Embrace the Continent

When asked to name the most powerful country in Korean history, everyone would undoubtedly answer "Goguryeo," and when asked to name the greatest monarch in our history, they would not hesitate to state "King Gwanggaeto." However, there is another country that achieved such glory—namely, the Balhae Empire, which ruled over a vast territory of 5,000 *li* (里)[1] in all directions. Nonetheless, the maps depicting the territorial extent of Balhae, even without reflecting changes over time, are strangely inconsistent. Some maps exclude the Liaodong area completely, while others include areas from Gangneung, Gangwon-do, and along the banks of the Amnok River to

---

[1] It is a unit of distance used in East Asian countries such as Korea, China, and Japan. It is equal to about 0.4 km.

Buyeo-bu. Yet another map shows the entire Liaodong (Kr. Yodong, 遼東) region within Balhae's sphere of influence.

Crisscross Manchuria, Embracing the People

Dae Joyeong, who had been forcefully relocated to Yingzhou (營州, present-day Chaoyang, Liaoning) after the fall of Goguryeo, took advantage of the revolt of Li Jinzhong and Son Wanying in 696 against the tyranny of the Yingzhou governor and led the Goguryeo refugees and the Malgal people across the Liao River. Thus began the epic journey to the land of Goguryeo. The Tang dynasty tried to appease Dae Joyeong's father, Geolgeoljungsang (乞乞仲象), by awarding him the title of Duke of Jinguo (震國公) and proclaimed the Malgal chief, Geolsabiu (乞四比羽), to Duke of Xuguo (許國公), but it also sent a large force of troops to pursue them. However, Dae Joyeong eventually established his kingdom, Jinguk, on Mt. Dongmo. This was a brilliant achievement for the discriminated-against and derided refugee people who had been forced to move to foreign places like Yingzhou and Shandong and escaped to mountainous regions following the loss of their homeland in 668. The Goguryeo people who had remained in their homeland and suffered all kinds of hardships, as well as the Malgals, many of whom had been subject to being buried alive for their collaboration with Goguryeo, gathered to join the new kingdom.

As the refugees streamed toward Mt. Dongmo, the reputation of Dae Joyeong further grew. With the opening of relations with the Turks and Silla, external threats also gradually diminished. Dae Joyeong, renowned for his "courage and skillful military operations," devoted himself to expanding the kingdoms's control over Manchuria, leading successful campaigns westward to Buyeo, eastward to Okjeo and Byeonhan, southward to Joseon[today's Liaoyang(遼陽)], and northward to Malgal.

The tang dynasty did not want to recognize Balhae's founding, but it sent an envoy named Cui Xin to Balhae, appointing Dae Joyoung as General of Jwahyowiwonoe (左驍尉員外大將軍), Balhae-Gunwang (渤海郡王), the Governor of Holhanju (忽汗州都督), and improving relations with Balhae. On one hand, the establishment of diplomatic relations between the Tang and Balhae not only ameliorated the hostile relations that had existed since the fall of Goguryeo, but on the other hand, it also signified that the world that had been unified under the Tang was once again divided into separate domains of the Tang and Balhae.

Conflict and Division, Followed by Unity

After King Mu, Dae Muye (大武藝), ascended to the throne, Balhae became even more powerful and its territorial dominion expanded. Historians noted in their records, "With significant territorial expansion, the northeastern barbarians became fearful and submitted. The term "northeastern barbarians" referred to the Heuksu Malgal (Ch. Heishui Mohe, 黑水靺鞨) living in the Heilong River (黑龍江) region. In 725, during the first negotiations between the Heuksu Malgal and the Tang dynasty, Balhae played a bridging role. Balhae also acted as an intermediary when the Heuksu Malgal sought the title of Tutun (吐屯, provincial governor) from the Turks.

However, at some point, a rift began to form between Balhae and the Heuksu Malgal. Seizing the opportunity, the Tang dynasty intervened and established its influence. Despite their previous efforts to improve relations with Balhae, the Tang dynasty actively fomented the split between Balhae and the Heuksu Malgal. The Heuksu Malgal, who were seeking to free themselves from Balhae's political influence, were inclined to accept the "loose-reign" (Kr. Gimi, Ch. Jimi, 羈縻) policy of the Tang, which suited their own interests. As the Tang dynasty's political maneuvers were exposed within a short period of time, the relationship between Balhae and the Tang, as well as between Balhae and the Heuksu Malgal, rapidly deteriorated.

> "In the beginning, the Heuksu Malgal contacted us to engage with the Tang dynasty, and even when they were seeking [the title of] Tutun from the Turks, they informed us first. However, now they fail to inform us of their current deal with the Tang dynasty, suggesting their intention to attack us from both sides together with the Tang."
>
> - *Jiu Tangshu* (舊唐書)

The Malgal tribes, originally called Mulgil (Ch. Wuji) in the region of Suksin (Ch. Sushen) during the period of the Northern Wei (北魏, 465-535), were 6,000 *li* to the northeast of the Tang capital Chang'an and consisted of seven tribes north of Goguryeo; the Songmal (粟末), Baekdol (伯咄), Angeogol (安車骨), Bulyeol (拂涅), Hosil (號室), Heuksu (黑水), Baeksan (白山). Among them, the Heuksu was the most powerful, and during its heyday, its domain extended from north to south, covering distances of 200 *li* or even 300 to 400 *li*, controlling 16 provinces. Additionally, the Malgal tribes in the provinces of Uru, Wolheui, and Cheolli grew into forces capable of negotiating with the central powers from time to time, although their exact locations have not been determined, unlike the provinces of Samo, Gulli, Gunseol, and Makyeogae.

King Mu of Balhae dispatched a swift military expedition led by Dae Munye and Im Ah (任雅) to subdue the Heuksu Malgal. Although there is no precise record of the outcome, we still can surmise that Balhae's offensive was thorough and severe for the following reasons. First, in a letter initiating diplomatic relations with Japan in 727, King Mu claimed that he expanded Balhae's territory to "2,000 *li* on all four sides," and that his kingdom "recovered the old lands of Goguryeo, and carried on the old customs of Buyeo." Second, such Malgal groups as the Wolheui (越喜), Bulyeol (拂涅), and Cheolli (鐵利), which had been under the influence of the Heuksu Malgal, stopped sending tribute to the Tang for ten years from 725 to 735, while the Heuksu Magal sent only one tributary mission to the Tang from 730 to 740. According to historical records, "the northeastern barbarians were scared and quickly submitted," and Balhae's territory "extended southward to connect with Silla, reaching the Wolheui Malgal and the northeastern Heuksu Malgal, covering a vast area of 2,000 *li* in all directions."

Constructing the Foundation of the Haedongseongguk

Balhae's territorial expansion continued during the reign of King Mun. When internal conflicts arose among the Western Turks, King Mun extended his influence over the Funie and Wolheui Malgals to the northeast. He then extended his influence further by expanding into the territory of the Cheolli Malgal, downstream of the Wusuli River, making it impossible for them to collaborate with the Tang dynasty. The success of King Mun's inroad into the Malgal groups can be surmised through the record of the *Shoku Nihongi* (續日本紀, 697-791, Chronicles of Japan, continued) about 1,100 people of Balhae and Cheoli naturalized into Japan in 748"

The circumstances under which Balhae expanded its power into the Malgal groups were not the same during the reigns of King Go, King Mu, and King Mun. The period of King Go saw the influx of the Malgal groups into the central power, since they cooperated with Dae Joyeong's founding of the new state, while the subsequent periods of King Mu and King Mun were marked by a stratification of the ruling class with both their separation and incorporation, thus posing a challenge to the central power. As its northern territories stabilized, Balhae turned its attention to Silla to the south. The record in the *Samguk sagi* that Silla built "Daegok Fortress for the first time" in Hwanghae-do, south of the Daedong River, indicates a defensive measure against Balhae, which had expanded its influence to the northern bank of the Daedong River. Balhae's expansion of its power into the Liaodong region can be proven by the following statements in the historical records: "Yelu Abaoji's (耶律阿保機) troops attacked the Liaodong (i.e., Balhae)" in the *Zizhi tongjian* (資治通鑑, Comprehensive Mirror to Aid in Government), "Dongjing (東京, the eastern capital of the Liao Dynasty) was Balhae's old territory" in the *Qidan Guozhi* (契丹國志, Records of the Khitan state), and "Liaoyang was blocked to the west" in the *Letters of the Central Office of Balhae, Addressed to the Bureau of Great Council of Japan*.

"The old territory of Suksin was established as Sanggyeong (上京), and its southern part was established as Junggyeong (中京). The old territory of Yemaek was designated as Donggyeong (東京), the old territory of Okjeo as Namgyeong (南京), and the old territory of Goryeo as the Seogyeong (西京)… The Buyeo-bu and Makhil-bu were established in the old territory of Buyeo, and the Jeongni-bu and Anbyeon-bu were established in the old territory of Eumnu. The Solbin-bu was established in the old territory of

Solbin, the Dongpyeong-bu in the old territory of Bulyeol, the Cheolli-bu in the old territory of Cheolli, and the Hoewon-bu and Anwon-bu in the old territory of Wolheui respectively. [Balhae's] region extended 5,000 *li*, its households numbered over 100,000, and its superior soldiers numbered tens of thousands."

- *Xin Tangshu* (新唐書)

During his 57-year reign, King Mun established borders with Silla and the Malgals and organized the administrative regions into 5 Gyeong (京, capital), 15 Bu (府, Provinces), and 62 Ju (州, county). In the years from 742 to 756 (the Tianbao era of Tang Emperor Xuanzong), he implemented a policy of moving the capital every year to efficiently govern the entire country, from the Central Capital Junggyeong to the Upper Capital Sanggyeong (located in the north), then to the Eastern Capital Dongyeong thus laying the foundation for the balanced and harmonious development of the nation. In addition, as the names of his era, *Daeheung* (大興, Great Rising) and *Boryeok* (寶曆, Valuable Era) suggest, King Mun attempted to restore people's livelihood on the basis of the expanded territory, laying the foundation for the kingdom's reputation as the Haedongseongguk (海東盛國, *Flourishing Kingdom of the East*). As a result, he was praised for "widely spreading royal enlightenment and achieving significant military accomplishments comparable to ancient sage kings such as Yu the Great (大禹), King Tang (湯) of Shang, and King Wen of Zhou (周文王)."

6.
The Imperial Status of Balhae, as Established by King Mun

Kim Jinkwang

Presuppositions when Considering the Historical Status of Balhae

There are different views on the historical status of Balhae. If Balhae is seen as a state founded by the "refugees of Goguryeo," then its status should be viewed as a "restoration state of Goguryeo" or a "state inheriting Goguryeo culture." In contrast, if it is considered to be a state founded by the Malgal, then its status should be determined based on its relationship with the Malgal. Furthermore, it is important to consider that many historical records about Balhae written in Chinese reflect the Sino-centric worldview. Therefore, attention should be paid to interpreting objective royal titles such as Wang (王), Gunwang (君王), and Gukwang (國王). In addition, we need to understand the subjective titles, such as Hwangsang (皇上, His Majesty the Emperor) and Seongin (聖人, Sacred Person) inscribed in the epitaphs of Princess

Jeonghye and Princess Jeonghyo, as well as the term Cheonson (天孫, Grandson of Heaven) in diplomatic documents sent to Japan.

Self-dentification as Grandson of Heaven

Contrary to the Chinese view of Balhae, various clues left by Balhae suggest that it possessed the characteristics of an imperial state. It is believed that Balhae attained its imperial status at least during the reign of King Mun, and this status was symbolized in its self-identification.

Clues to this can be found in the *Shoku Nihongi*. King Mun declared his kingdom as successor to the old lands of Goguryeo and the customs of Buyeo, referred to himself as the king of Goryeo (i.e., Goguryeo), and pronounced himself Cheonson, Grandson of Heaven. In particular, his self-image as Grandson of Heaven echoed the tradition of King Dongmyeong of Buyeo, and King Jumong and King Gwanggaeto of Goguryeo identifying themselves as "Son of the Sun and Moon." This was destructive enough to cause diplomatic friction with Japan.

Imperial Terminology of Emperor and Empress

The epitaphs of Princess Jeonghye and Princess Jeonghyo contain the imperial terminology such as "His Majesty the Emperor" in a sentence "[His majesty the Emperor], saddened by the death of the princess, did not hold the morning audience." This term refers to the father of the princess, King Mun, and indicates the title used to address the king in Balhae's court. However, Chinese imperial terms such as "Huangdi (皇帝, emperor)" were not found anywhere. Instead, similarly to how the emperor was addressed as "Bixia (陛下, your majesty)" in the Chinese court, Balhae used the term "Giha (基下, below your majesty)."

King Mun was also addressed as "Sacred Person." Since this term conventionally referred to the sage-emperors Yao (堯) and Shun (舜), comparing King Mun to these revered figures indicates that his status in Balhae was highly respected. In Balhae, "Sacred (聖)" was one of the titles used when addressing the king in person. Even in diplomatic documents where Balhae presented its own status, King Mun referred to himself as the king of Goryeo (i.e., Goguryeo).

Another symbolic title was "Great King (大王)." Examples of "Great King" can be found in *Cefu yuangui* (冊府元龜), saying "the Great King of Balhae, [Dae] Muye, sent his Crown Prince [Dae] Dorihaeng (大都利行) to attend the audience [at the Tang court]," The title is found in a statement of the *Nihon ishi* (日本逸史) that "Heaven became angry and Grandfather the Great King passed away on the fourth day of the third month of the fifty-seventh year of the Daeheung era." In addition, a royal seal inscribed with "Great King of Balhae" was discovered in Sanggyeong of Balhae. Since the Goguryeo rulers sought to identify themselves as the "Son of the Sun and Moon" while using the title "Great King" instead of "Emperor" to the outside world, the

Balhae rulers' use of "Great King" had the same connotation as that of the Goguryeo rulers.

Another imperial title of the Balhae court was *Hwanghu* (皇后, Empress). This title was confirmed in 2005 by the discovery of the epitaph of the queen of King Mun (Empress Hyoeui) and the queen of King Gan (Empress Sunmok) in the Mt. Longtou tomb complex where Princess Jeonghyo was buried. To date, this title has not been found in any other known historical documents or inscriptions. For example, in the *Jiu Wudaishi* (舊五代史), the king's wife was called Noble Queen (貴妃) and the king's mother was called Great Queen (太妃). The above evidence that the queen of Balhae was called Empress allows us to infer by extension that in the Balhae court, the king was called Emperor, the royal court was called Imperial Court, and the royal capital was called Imperial Capital.

Use of Independent Era Names

Another clue regarding Balhae's imperial status lies in its era names. Balhae's independent era names were confirmed by the tombs of Princess Jeonghye, the second daughter of King Mun, and Princess Jeonghyo, the fourth daughter of King Mun, discovered in 1949 and 1981 respectively. In addition to the era name Daeheung, which can be found in the *Jiu Tangshu* and the *Xin Tangshu*, an additional era name Boryeok was also used. From a historical record stating that "an independent era name was privately used" when King Mu ascended the throne, it can be inferred that era names were used even before that time. The Chinese record suggests that Balhae used its own era names adopted by the succeeding kings after the death of Dae Joyeong in 719, without the approval of the Chinese dynasty, implying a lack of political legitimacy from the Chinese perspective.

Traditionally, only emperors were allowed to adopt new era names, but some Korean kingdoms before and after Balhae had their own era names. Goguryeo's King Gwanggaeto used the era name Yeongnak, and Taehwa was inscribed on the seven-branched knife of Baekje. In Silla, King Beopheung established the era name Geonwon and King Jinheung had multiple era names of Gaeguk Daechang, Hongje, and Geonbok, while Queen Jindeok used the era name Taehwa. Gungye of Later Goguryeo also used era names such as Mutae, Seongchaek, Sudeokmanse, and Jeonggae, and Goryeo's King Gwangjong used the era names Junpung and Gwangdeok.

However, King Mun of Balhae went a step further and used not only the era name Daehyeong, but also Boryeok during his reign. This was two years before the diplomatic conflict with Japan triggered by his claim to Grandson of Heaven in 777. While there are instances where an emperor established multiple era names, it was more common for emperors to use only one. Since the initiation of a new era was often associated with significant transitional periods in governance, political circumstances, or religious aspirations, King

Mun's change of the era name can be understood as marking a crucial shift in the policy and operation of the kingdom.

The Royal Tomb Institution

The tomb institution in China can be traced back to a statement in the *Shiji* (史記, Records of the Grand Historian) that the "[royal tomb institution] had been in place in the era of King Yu (禹) of the Xia (夏) dynasty." In Korea, we can also confirm that this system was established in the Goguryeo period through various historical materials. Since the term neung (陵) refers to the tomb of a king or queen, the tombs named 'Jin-neung' or '☐-neung' are sure to be those of a certain king or queen, even if their real owners are unknown. Moreover, as the term won (園) marked the tomb of princes and princesses in the Joseon dynasty, the tombs of Balhae's princes and princesses were also likely named '☐-won' or '☐☐-won.' Since a royal cemetery named 'Jin-neung' had already been constructed prior to the death of Princess Jeonghye, it can be inferred that the royal tomb institution of Balhae was established around that time. The 2005 archaeological findings show that the tomb of Empress Sunmok was named "☐-neung" in 829 under the reign of the tenth king, King Seon (Dae Insu), suggesting that Balhae had developed another status symbol of the imperial state.

Institution of the Crown Prince

The epitaphs of the two Balhae princesses refer to them as the sisters of the Donggung (東宮, crown prince). The term Donggung generally refers to the crown prince, and it also denotes the palace where the crown prince resides. In ancient times, the Donggung system was established to educate, support, and protect the crown prince, thus ensuring the prolonged continuation of the imperial line. It seems that Balhae developed the institution of the crown prince by the year 777 and the accompanying education in preparation for raising him as the future emperor. Balhae not only referred to its king as Emperor, but had also established supporting systems that would solidify his status. Balhae's efforts to raise its status to that of an imperial state were made possible by its continuous territorial expansion, population growth, and cultural integration since its founding, and especially in the King Mun era and onward. Thanks to these efforts, Balhae came to be called the Haedongseongguk, the *Flourishing Kingdom of the East*, as it formed the Southern and Northern Kingdoms with Silla.

7.
Reasons for Balhae's Sea Campaign against the Tang at Dengzhou

Kwen Eunju

Rise of the Northern Peoples and Balhae's Diplomacy

In the late 7th century, the northern tribes flourished and actively engaged in various activities in Northeast Asia. It was in this context that Balhae was founded in 698. During its establishment, Balhae interacted with various northern tribes such as the Turks, the Khitans, and the Malgal, forming a resistance against the Tang dynasty. Due to its rapid growth and alliances with these northern tribes, Balhae became a major target of the Tang dynasty. Paradoxically, this situation also became the backdrop for the easing of tensions between Balhae and the Tang dynasty in the 710s.

Balhae entered a period of relative stability about ten years after its founding. A buffer zone called Liaoxi (遼西) existed between Balhae and the Tang dynasty, which also served as a buffer in its relationship

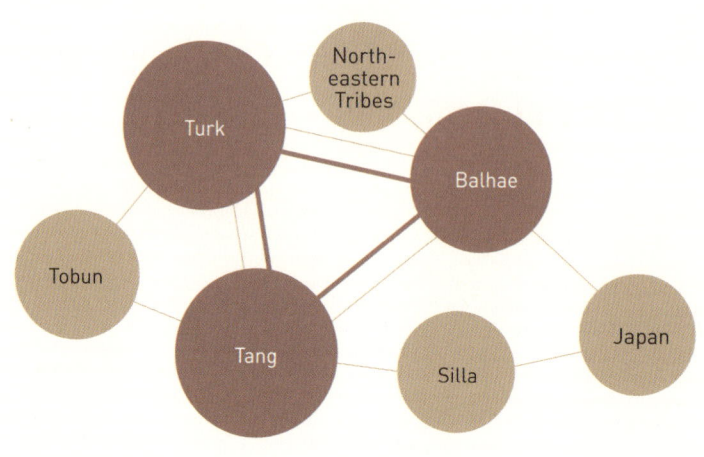

Political and Military Relations among States of Northeast Asia from 698 AD to the First Half of the 8th Century.

with the Turks. As a result, Balhae was somewhat free from the direct influence of the two dominant powers in Northeast Asia at the time, allowing it to be more flexible in its foreign relations.

In 713, the Tang dynasty sent envoys to establish diplomatic relations with Balhae as part of their efforts to weaken the alliance of northern tribes. From that point on, tensions between the two countries eased considerably. However, the primary focus of Balhae's diplomacy continued to be dealing with the northern tribes.

Starting in the 720s, Balhae actively engaged in territorial expansion, and the northern peoples began to gather forces against the Tang dynasty again. During this period, Balhae's relationship with the northern peoples strengthened, while tensions with the Tang dynasty resurfaced. Finally, in 732, Balhae crossed the sea and attacked the Tang mainland, specifically the city of Dengzhou(登州).

Beginning of Estrangement between Balhae and the Tang

The first incident that revealed discord between Balhae and the Tang dynasty occurred in 720. In the fall of that year, when the Xi (奚) and the Khitans in the Liaoxi region allied themselves in rebellion against the Tang dynasty, the Tang turned to Balhae for military assistance to put down them. At the same time, the Tang also faced attacks from the Turks in the northwest region, which was directly related to an uprising in Liaoxi. However, Balhae did not respond to the Tang's request for support. Consequently, the Tang forces suffered a major defeat in the Liaoxi region, and the northeastern defense line retreated significantly southward from Yingzhou (營州).

As a result of this incident, the Tang dynasty began to be suspicious regarding the relationship between Balhae and the northern peoples. In addition, the Heuksu Malgal, who felt threatened by Balhae's territorial expansion during King Mu's reign, approached the Tang dynasty, and the Tang tried to use them as a counterbalance to Balhae. At the same time, Balhae's southern neighbor, Silla, was also strengthening its diplomatic ties with the Tang dynasty. Balhae responded by subjugating the Heuksu Malgal in 726 and opening relations with Japan in 727 to put pressure on Silla.

In the meantime, an incident further escalated tensions between Balhae and the Tang dynasty. Dae Munye (大門藝), a younger brother of Balhae's King Mu, opposed the punitive expedition against the Heuksu Malgal and sought refuge in the Tang dynasty. Since the vendetta between Dae Munye and King Mu could have been used by the Tang to create a serious rift within the Balhae kingdom, King Mu asked the Tang to kill Dae Munye, but the Tang refused. Furthermore, the death of Dae Dorihaeng (大都利行), the son of King Mu, who had stayed in the Tang as an imperial guard, complicated the relations between the two countries, because it involved the succession issue of Balhae. Despite these complications, Balhae refrained from direct confrontation with the Tang and instead sought to resolve the issues through diplomatic negotiations, at least for some time.

Balhae's Attack on Dengzhou and the Anti-Tang War of the Northern Peoples

The reason why Balhae sent Jang Munhyu (張文休) to attack Dengzhou of the Tang in 732 was largely influenced by the changing circumstances in the buffer zone, the Liaoxi region. The 730s saw the resumption of the anti-Tang war of the northern peoples. In the fifth month of 730, the Khitans led by Ketugan (可突干), along with the Xi, submitted themselves to the Turks and began their attacks against the

Chapter 3 TERRITORIAL EXPANSION 69

Battlefields of Balhae Against the Tang Dynasty in the 730s

Tang. Their large-scale rebellion forced the Tang to raise large forces for battles that lasted for several months from the sixth month to the autumn of 730.

The existence of the buffer zone in the Liaoxi region played a crucial role in helping Balhae to found a new state and expand its power. The stability in the Liaoxi region provided Balhae with a flexible diplomatic environment. Moreover, the anti-Tang stance of Ketugan in control of the region worked to Balhae's advantage in its territorial expansion in the 720s and dominance over the Malgal in the northeast.

However, if the Liaoxi regions controlled by the Khitans fell into the hands of the Tang, that would mean the disappearance of the buffer zone and Balhae would face a direct confrontation with the Tang. This situation would also weaken Balhae's control of the Malgal peoples. Therefore, Balhae sent its last emissary to the Tang in the tenth month of 731, thus ending diplomatic efforts and resorting to military actions in concert with the northern peoples to resolve the conflicts with the Tang.

Starting in the first month of 732, the Tang launched large-scale military operations to suppress the rebellions of the Khitans and the Xi. In the early third month, the Tang achieved significant victories, causing the leader of the Xi and over 5,000 members of the ordu (Ch. zhang, 帳) to surrender to the Tang. As a result, the anti-Tang forces were temporarily weakened. This was when Balhae took the opportunity to attack the Tang. In the ninth month, Balhae attacked the Tang's rear base at Dengzhou to support the cornered Khitans' forces.

After that, Balhae also participated in the battle of Mt. Madou (馬都山, near modern-day Qinhuangdao in Hebei), which took place in the third (leap) month of 733. Balhae, along with the Khitans and the Turks, engaged in battles against the Tang dynasty here. The Balhae forces inflicted so much damage that the Tang records say that the Balhae troops slaughtered the entire city. It was not until the Tang's Wu Chengci (烏承玼) built a fortification of 400 *li* long in 734 that the Tang refugees returned to the city. Balhae proved to be a significant military force during its participation in the conflict.

The Post-War Period

The anti-Tang War, which began in the Liaoxi region in 730, swept through northern China (Ch. Huabei, 華北) and the Shandong area, and continued until 734. However, the anti-Tang alliance peaked at the battle of Mt. Madou and began to weaken and disintegrate. Unable to suppress the anti-Tang forces after Balhae's participation in the war, the Tang dynasty adopted a strategy of creating splits within the Khitans' power struggle. They instigated Li Guozhe (李過折) to kill Ketugan and his followers, and to submit to the Tang dynasty.

As for Balhae, the Tang granted sovereignty to Silla over the south of the Daedong River in early 735, allowing Silla to check Balhae from the south. At this time, the Turkic Empire began to collapse with the death of Bilge Khan, the central figure of the anti-Tang coalition, in 734. Consequently, the anti-Tang coalition of the northern peoples naturally disintegrated.

However, the dissolution of the anti-Tang coalition did not substantially damage Balhae. With the passage of time, the issue of succession to the throne triggered by the death of Dae Dorihaeng was settled, as the third king, King Mun (Dae Heummu) had been established firmly in Balhae. Dae Munye was no longer a threat to the crown. The disappearance of Dae Munye in the Tang's records after the war indicates that the Tang did not find him to have any value in its dealings with Balhae. In addition, even after the collapse of the anti-Tang alliance of the northern peoples, the Tang never fully regained control of the Liaoxi region. Liaoxi consequently remained a buffer zone to the advantage of Balhae.

Interestingly, only Balhae and Silla benefited from the war. Balhae was able to strengthen its internal cohesion and royal authority through military activities in the Hebei and Liaoxi regions. They also expanded control over the neighboring Malgal groups, and laid the foundation for the reign of the third king, Mun. In the meantime, Silla's late participation in the anti-Balhae attack did not bring about any noteworthy results. Nonetheless, Silla began to secure the area south of the Daedong River, which had remained a power vacuum since the end of the Silla-Tang war (668-676), and pushed forward with its territorialization process.

8.
Japan's Plan to Subjugate Silla

Kim Jinkwang

Recurring Specter of "Conquest of Korea"

A Korean TV drama named *Mr. Sunshine* depicts how Meiji Japan, following in the footstpes of the Western imperial powers, took over the Korean Empire. This drama might have enjoyed a high rating among Korean viewers because it echoed a recent series of absurd statements by some Japanese officials about sensitive issues such as the dissolution of the 'Reconciliation and Healing Foundation' and the Korean Supreme Court's rulings on forced laborer compensation.

The idea of Japan's Jeong-Han non (征韓論, J. Seikanron, Conquest of Korea) was not limited to Korean history of the late nineteenth century. Further back in history, Hideyoshi Toyotomi (豐臣秀吉), who unified Japan during the Warring States Period, instigated the Imjin War against Joseon (i.e., Korea) to quell domestic discontent, relying on the support of merchants in the Osaka and Sakai regions. Even longer ago, there was the "Plan to Subjugate Silla," in which Japan announced their intention to conquer Silla. This plan was triggered by diplomatic friction during the reign of King Gyeongdeok of Silla. Going back even further in history, based on their interpretation of the *Nihon shoki* (日本書紀), some Japanese scholars claimed that in the 4th century the Yamato (大和) regime of ancient Japan established a Japanese-controlled government in Mimana (任那), which was Gaya (伽倻) in southern Korea, and ruled for approximately 200 years. The Seikanron or the Conquest of Korea, as a political ideology to emphasize the superiority of Japan over Korea, has recurred throughout the history of Korea-Japan relations like a resurrected specter.

Mid-Eighth-Century Northeast Asia: An Eye of a Typhoon

The mid-eighth century, when Balhae was at the peak of its prosperity, saw a great disturbance in the Northeast Asian region because of the impact of the An Lushan (安祿山) rebellion. An Lushan, who had been defeated by Yang Guozhong over the position of former Chancellor Li Linfu, led rebel forces and occupied Luoyang (洛陽), forcing Emperor Xuanzong (玄宗) of the Tang to flee to the Sichuan region. The once-thriving Tang dynasty, known for its "Kaiyuan Era of Prosperity (開元之治)," suddenly found itself trampled under the hooves of invading foreign forces. Due to the uncertainties in Northeast Asia at that time, Balhae, Silla, and Japan were on alert and closely watching the situation of the Tang dynasty. A record from this time states, "At the outbreak of the An Lushan Rebellion in 756, a liaison officer of the Pinglu Army, Xu Guidao (徐歸道), sent a magistrate of Liucheng County, Zhang Yuanjian (張元澗), to request the mobilization of Balhae's cavalry forces. But [King Mun] remained skeptical and did not move [his armies]." Unprecedented turmoil erupted in Northeast Asia, making it difficult to predict in which direction it would spread.

Seeking Justification for War

The aftermath of the An Lushan Rebellion was not confined to the Tang dynasty. As Japan plotted an attack on Silla, unexpected tensions emerged among the three Northeast Asian states: Balhae, Silla, and Japan. Fujiwara Nakamaro's (藤原仲麻呂, 706-764) plan to attack Silla in the years 759-762 was triggered by Silla King Gyeongdeok's expulsion of a Japanese envoy for his rudeness in 753. The reign of King Gyeongdeok, during which the incident occurred, was a period of political, social, and cultural prosperity for Silla. King Gyeongdeok pursued reform policies based on stable royal authority and established a strong centralized legal system. He simultaneously sought to improve Silla's external status by exploring cooperation with the Tang dynasty and Balhae. On the military front, he implemented military reforms after the An-Shi rebellion in China, and attempted to expand military capacity by establishing a naval defense system. However, these actions of King Gyeongdeok of Silla caused friction with Japan.

Silla's friction with Japan was not only due to the strong domestic and foreign policies and military expansion during the reign of King Gyeongdeok. Diplomatic relations between the two countries had been deteriorating since the reign of King Seongdeok, and there were signs of imminent armed conflict. As a result, in 722, Silla mobilized over 40,000 troops in the southeastern region of Gyeongju to build fortifications. In 731, Silla repelled an invasion by 300 Japanese warships along the east coast, and in 732, they strengthened their city defenses. Finally, when Silla's envoy to Japan, Sangjeong Kim, referred to his kingdom as "Wangseongguk (王城國, the kingdom of the king's castle)," Japan requested the protocol of a vassal state to Silla. After Silla refused, Japan launched the "conquest of Silla" plan.

Japan's Strengthening of the Military

The "conquest of Silla" plan was formulated a year after the An-Shi rebellion. It was led by Fujiwara Nakamaro, who played a leading role in restoring the legal system (*ritsuryō* system) based on the Tang model during the reign of Emperor Junnin of Japan. Some scholars suggest that this plan was aimed at diverting domestic discontent within Japan, which involved criticisms of Fujiwara's political autocracy, to external territories.

After suffering defeat in battles against Silla, Japan took a series of measures. In 731, the military headquarters in the capital area and the provincial garrisons along the western and southern coastal areas were established. Large fortresses were built in areas directly facing Silla, such as the Dazai-fu (太宰府) and San'indō (山陰道), and military commissioners were dispatched to the eastern and western coastal areas. Furthermore, a military manual in preparation for outside attack was compiled.

In 756, Ito fortress (怡土城) was built in northern Kyushu. Dazaifu was ordered to construct a shipyard and factories to build warships and manufacture weaponry. In the sixth month of 759, a manual for mobilizing armies was compiled, and in the eighth month of the same year, the plan to conquer Silla was reported to the court. On the diplomatic front, a liaison officer Tamori Ono (小野田守) was dispatched to Balhae seeking military collaboration, and he was soon followed by envoys in 759 and 760. Moreover, in 761, they trained interpreters from the Silla ethnic group to participate in the expeditionary forces.

Broken Dreams, Shattered Trust

The result of the "conquest of Silla" plan remains uncertain. This is because Balhae had to prepare for the possibility of invasion by the Khitans as it expanded its influence into the Liaodong region, and the relations between Silla and Balhae had shifted to peaceful interactions. It is true that Balhae made more contacts with Japan in the mid-eighth century, yet it seems likely that Balhae's increased contacts with Japan were motivated by meeting its domestic economic needs rather than by participating in a joint attack against Silla with Japan.

The "conquest of Silla" plan was last mentioned in an account in 762 that "a ceremonial gift was offered to the Kashii shrine (香椎廟) in the hope of good training of the soldiers to be sent to punish Silla." The fact that nothing else was heard about the plan suggests that it was not enacted. In addition, the power struggle between Emperor Junnin and the retired Empress Kōken further weakened the momentum behind the "conquest of Silla" plan, and the policy toward Silla underwent a significant change after the restoration of Empress Kōken. The policy shift can be seen as a practical decision to adapt to the restructured order in Northeast Asia.

It cannot be denied that the "conquest of Silla" plan was triggered by diplomatic friction between Silla and Japan. However, the reconfigured international relations after the An-Shi rebellion created an environment in which Japan had no choice but to abandon the plan. Ultimately, the "conquest of Silla" plan was a product of the political frustrations of hardliners such as Fujiwara Nakamaro who sought to advance their political agenda, internal power struggles within the Japanese royal court, and international conflicts arising from the upheaval of the An-Shi rebellion.

9.
Reasons for Moving the Capital Four Times

Kwen Eunju

Frequent Moves of the Capital: A Key to Understanding the History of Balhae

In 2004, there was a heated issue in South Korea - namely, the enactment of the "Special Measures Act for the Construction of a New Administrative Capital" and the subsequent ruling by the Constitutional Court that this act was unconstitutional. The capital has been the seat of national authority from ancient times to the present, serving as the focal point for politics, administration, military, economy, and culture. Moving the capital is called *cheondo* (遷都). The New Administrative Capital Act included not only the relocation of administrative agencies, but also the relocation of the presidential office and the legislative body of the National Assembly, making it a kind of cheondo. The Constitutional Court of the Republic of Korea ruled the law unconstitutional, on the grounds that the fact that Seoul is the "capital" of South Korea falls under the category of "customary constitution" and that moving the capital without a national referendum is unconstitutional. As a result, the "Special Law on the Administrative City Construction" was enacted, leading to the relocation of many central administrative agencies to Sejong City. Nevertheless, Seoul remains the capital of South Korea.

Looking at the series of events surrounding the issue of the capital's relocation, one can speculate that relocating the capital is indeed a challenging undertaking. Although many people still support the idea of moving the capital, there are also many who oppose it. The reasons for opposition include the astronomical economic and social costs associated with the relocation of the capital, but underneath these reasons lies the intense divergence of interests among groups centered on the location of the capital.

The problems and conflicts arising from the relocation of the capital were also present in pre-modern times. Relocating the capital was possible only under certain circumstances - for example, when the circumstances were urgent or when there was enough power to carry it out. The former was often caused by war or internal rebellion, while the latter circumstances occurred due to factors such as territorial expansion, the establishment of a strong monarchy, increases in productivity, or social development.

During its 230-year rule, Balhae underwent four capital relocations in the following order: Mt. Dongmo or Guguk (舊國) to Junggyeong(Central Capital), to Sanggyeong (Upper Capital), to Donggyeong (Eastern Capital), back to Sanggyeong. It is true that Goguryeo and Baekje also moved their capital several times, but this pattern of Balhae was unique considering its relatively short existence.

Location of the First Capital of Balhae: Mt. Dongmo (Guguk)

Dae Joyeong established a fortress on Mt. Dongmo (東牟山), a location in the former borderland of Goguryeo, as the place where Balhae was founded. Mt. Dongmo is believed to be today's Chengshanzishan in Dunhua City, Jilin-sheng, China. Although the mountain is not very high, it stands prominently in the Dunhua basin, providing a panoramic view in all directions for defense against enemies. About 4 kilometers to the east is the headwaters of the Mudan River, while the Dashi River flows north of the mountain, forming a natural moat.

The early capital was called Guguk, meaning the original or home country. Mt. Dongmo, which was chosen for military rather than administrative reasons, was not an ideal place to build a full-fledged palace. It was only after the state had stabilized somewhat that a capital was built on the plains.

It is believed that the ruins of Yong-sheng or the site of the Aodong fortress was most likely the site for the palace on flatland. The ruins of Yong-sheng are located two kilometers west of the Mt. Liuding

Relocations of Balhae's Capitals

Tomb Complex, which was a cemetery for early royal members and aristocrats of Balhae. The site of Aodong fortress is located in today's Dunhua City, where artifacts from Balhae have been recovered. Recent discoveries at the remains of the Jin (金) - era fortresses also suggest that they may have been the site of Balhae's early palace, but more evidence is needed. Although it is not possible to confirm the

Mt. Dongmo

exact location of Balhae's flatland capital, it is clear that it was in the Dunhua area in the vicinity of the Mt. Liuding Tomb Complex.

Junggyeong of Balhae

As Balhae expanded its territory and kept growing, it was necessary to build a new capital, Sanggyeong, and the capital was moved there. According to the geography section (地理志) in the *Xin Tangshu*, however, Junggyeong, which was located in Hyeonzhou (顯州) of Hyeondeok-bu, was Balhae's capital during the Tianbao (天寶) era (742-756) of Tang Emperor Xuanzong.

If we take these records at face value, the upper limit for the year 742 and the lower limit for the year 756 would be when Junggyeong was the capital of Balhae. King Mun, the third king of Balhae, moved the capital three times during his reign: first from Guguk to Junggyeong, then from Junggyeong to Sanggyeong, and later to Donggyeong. It has been argued that Junggyeong relocation took place during the reign of King Mu, or that King Mu planned the relocation and King Mun carried it out.

There were four main reasons for moving the capital to Junggyeong. First, Junggyeong was considered more strategically stable in terms of national defense and had higher agricultural productivity than Guguk. Second, it served as a place to unite the Goguryeo refugees. Third, it was convenient for facilitating external interactions. Fourth, it was seen as a temporary capital to prepare for the eventual move to Sanggyeong.

The site of Junggyeong is considered to be in today's Xigucheng, Helong Prefecture, Jilin-sheng, China. The structure of the fortress is quite similar to Sanggyeong's inner fortress and Donggyeong (Baliancheng), and they share commonalities in construction materials. There are many Balhae historical sites nearby, including the Mt. Yongdu tomb complex where the tomb of Princess Jeonghyo (the fourth daughter of King Mun) was discovered, the Hanamdun fortress, the Haeran fortress, the Hanamdun tomb complex, and the Bukdae tomb complex.

Move to Sanggyeong and the An-Shi rebellion

Balhae finally relocated its capital to Sanggyeong in the 19th year of Daeheung (Great Rising) era of King Mun (755). Sanggyeong was located in today's Ningan City, Heilongjiang-sheng, China, on a wide and flat basin surrounded by the Mudan River. There are many Balhae historical sites in the area, such as the Samryeongdun tomb complex, Hongjuneojang tomb complex, and Daemokdan mountain fortress.

Interestingly, the relocation to Sanggyeong coincided with the rebellion of An Lushan and Sh Simingi (755-763) in the Tang dynasty. For this reason, some speculate that the move to Sanggyeong was an attempt to escape the disturbances caused by the rebellions. However, considering the national strength of Balhae at that time, it is difficult to fully accept the claim that they moved the capital to avoid the early stages of rebellions in China.

To begin with, the rebellion covered mainly the northern (Hubei) region of China, and the rebel forces advanced southward. The control over the Pinglu military prefecture in the Liaoxi region next to Balhae had already been in the hands of a pro-Tang faction for quite some time. But after a while, when the Xi tribes took control over the region, the Pinglu military prefecture was relocated to Shandong, thus leaving the Liaoxi region out of the Tang's control. Furthermore, Sanggyeong was located on a vast plain. It may have been suitable as a capital when surrounding military stability was secured, but the site may not have been suitable for sudden relocation due to external crises.

Balhae achieved rapid growth starting with its first ruler, King Dae Joyeong, and the second ruler, King Mu, actively expanded its territory. In the early reign of the third ruler, King Mun, a certain degree of subjugation was achieved over the Malgal region to the north. King Mun also adopted the culture and institutions of the Tang dynasty to structure the ruling system. The relocation of the capital to Sanggyeong was a deliberate move to efficiently govern the vast territory and was part of a planned effort to accommodate Balhae's elevated status.

It is possible that the An-Shi rebellion was used to speed up the transfer of the capital to Sanggyeong or to soften any resistance that might arise in the early stages of the relocation of the capital by emphasizing the external threat. However, the move of the capital to Sanggyeong was primarily the result of progress during an approximately 60-year period since the founding of Balhae, and it was not aimed to escape turmoil in other countries.

Reasons Behind the Move to Donggyeong

After the capital was moved to Sanggyeong, Balhae began to develop into an imperial state in the 770s. However, there was another capital transfer to Donggyeong around 785. Donggyeong was located in modern Baliancheng, Hunchun City, Jilin-sheng, China. There are also many Balhae historical remains in the vicinity of Donggyeong.

The decision to move the capital from Sanggyeong, which had optimal conditions as the capital, to Donggyeong in the eastern borderland has long puzzled many historians. A widely accepted theory is that in the last years of King Mun's reign, divisive forces challenged the centralizing power of the king, who resorted to the relocation of the capital to neutralize such forces. However, there is no confirmed evidence of internal conflicts. Therefore, it is more reasonable to consider the decision to move the capital to Donggyeong as an agreement between King Mun and the central aristocrats.

Why did they decide to move the capital to Donggyeong at that time and what was their intention? It should be noted that around the same time, the Tang dynasty was troubled by rebellions by provincial military garrisons (Ch. fanzhen, 藩鎭), while the Uighur (Ch. Hoeheul, 回紇) was unstable due to its campaign to purge the Sogdian merchants who had led the country's international trade. The unsettling situations in the Tang and the Uighur made it difficult for Balhae to conduct normal exchanges with the countries to its west. Balhae adopted a policy where the royal authority controlled foreign trade and, as a measure to control local subordinate groups, it allowed them to participate in foreign trade. However, this policy became a risk factor for Balhae under the changed international circumstances.

Therefore, it is very likely that King Mun was trying to prevent the possible exodus of subjugated ethnic groups due to the chaos in the western regions and to expand his territory to the eastern coastal area. The decision to return to his earlier era name (Daeheung, meaning Great Rising) may also reflect these circumstances. The historical remains of Balhae found in the Russian Yeonhaeju clearly indicate that the territory of Balhae expanded significantly during this period. This may be related to the relocation of the capital to Donggyeong.

After the death of King Mun in 793, internal conflicts arose when Dae Woneui (大元義), who was not King Mun's direct heir, took the throne. Dae Woneuii seemed to have gained influence after the transfer of the capital to Donggyeong. However, Dae Woneui was immediately overthrown by Balhae's central aristocrats (Kr. guk-in 國人), and the legitimate successor Dae Hwayeo (大華璵, i.e., King Seong) ascended the throne. In other words, these internal conflicts occurred after the transfer of the capital to Donggyeong.

Sanggyeong: Another Center of the East Asian World

King Seong, who had overcome the internal strife in Donggyeong and ascended to the throne, moved the capital back to Sanggyeong in 795. From that time until the fall of Balhae, Sanggyeong was the capital of Balhae.

The territorial expansion of Balhae continued after the capital was moved to Sanggyeong. In particular, King Seon (r. 818-830) brought

Chapter 3 TERRITORIAL EXPANSION   89

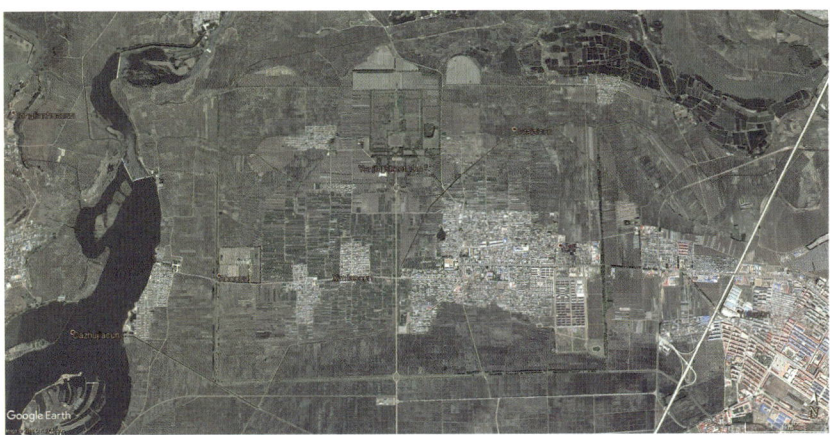

Satellite Photo of Sanggyeong

A View of Sanggyeong Palace Site from the Obong Tower

the various northern tribes under control and extended his power toward Silla. Sanggyeong, placed at the center of vast lands, was an ideal seat of government to control Balhae's large territory. From there, the succeeding kings in the ninth century and onward put their efforts into building a culturally prosperous state that would be called the Haedongseongguk, the *Flourishing Kingdom of the East*. Sanggyeong functioned as the heartland of Balhae, which became another prosperous empire in the East Asian world.

CHAPTER 4
ESTABLISHING AUTHORITY

10.
Emergence of Suryeong and Territorial Expansion

Kim Jinkwang

In the historical records of Balhae, such as the *Jiu Tangshu* (舊唐書) and *Xin Tangshu* (新唐書), the most prominent figures are Goguryeo refugees and the Malgal. This probably led to a tendency to understand Balhae as a dual system of the ruling elites consisting of Goguryeo remnants versus the subordinate classes of the Malgal peoples. Nonetheless, many questions are still not fully answered, such as who the Malgal peoples were in the first place, whether they were ethnically different from the ancestors of Koreans, what roles they played in Balhae, and how they were integrated into the central administration.

It is generally held, especially among Chinese scholars, that the Malgal (Ch. Mohe) can be placed into an ethnic succession line of Suksin (Ch. Sushen) → Eumnu (Ch. Yilou) → Mulgil (Ch. Wuji) → Malgal → Jurchen → Manchu. Contrastingly, a newer opinion exists, according to which the term Malgal was a pejorative or general term to refer to the border peoples of Goguryeo. Given the broad stretches of the settlements of the Malgal peoples, and analyses of individual cases where the term was used, it seems more convincing to see the term Malgal as a pejorative and generic reference to the peoples residing away from Balhae's central administration system. According to the *Xin Tangshu*, which refers to the founder of Balhae as Songmal Malgal, Songmal means the Songmal River (Ch. Sumojiang, present-day Sungari River or the Songhua River, 松花江)). Then, Songmal Malgal could refer to the "Malgal people living near the Songmal River." Moreover, if Malgal is considered a derogatory term, it can be understood as something similar to "country bumpkin." The same interpretation can be applied to Heuksu Malgal and Buyu Malgal.

In the establishment and growth of Balhae, however, the Malgal became a key force in foreign affairs. Commonly referred to as suryeong (首領), meaning leaders, they demonstrated their prominence during interactions with the Tang dynasty and Japan. Needless to say, the driving force that allowed these people to become a core strength of Balhae was closely related to the growth of Balhae after its founding.

The Dynamics between Balhae and the Malgal

In 696, Dae Joyeong escaped from Yingzhou (營州), crossed the Liao River (遼河), and defeated the Tang general Li Kaigu (李楷固) at

Tianmen Pass (天門嶺) before he established a new state named Jinguk around Mt. Dongmo (東牟山) in 698. The new state, later called Balhae, was established 30 years after the fall of Goguryeo in 668 by the Goguryeo remnants who had been relocated to Yingzhou and the Malgal peoples led by Geolsabiu (乞四比羽). With each step toward Mt. Dongmo, people from various backgrounds joined the ranks of Balhae, expanding the influence of the state. However, the constant threat of suppression by the Tang dynasty required the nation to ally itself not only with the Turks (突厥), but also with Silla.

The expansion of Balhae's territory would not have been possible without the outstanding military leadership of Dae Joyeong, renowned for his "courage and skillful military operations." However, the main reason for his achievements, such as "obtaining the kingdoms of Buyeo, Okjeo, Byeonhan, Joseon, and Haebuk," lay in the improvement of relations with the Tang dynasty, especially in gaining international recognition of the founding of his nation. The Tang dynasty sent a middle-ranking official, Zhang Xingji (張行岌), to confer an imperial title on Dae Joyeong in 705. In 713, fifteen years after the founding of Balhae, the Tang dynasty further established diplomatic relations with Balhae by sending another middle-ranking official, Cui Xin, to invest Dae Joyeong as the king of Balhae.

Balhae continued to expand its territory. In the process, it subjugated the Heuksu Malgal who had distanced themselves from Balhae and were leaning toward the Tang dynasty. The peoples of the northeastern region feared Balhae and willingly became subdued subjects. As a result, historical records describe its area as "bordering Silla in the south, reaching the Wolheui Malgal in the west, and extending to the Heuksu Malgal in the northeast, stretching about 2,000 *li* in all directions."

The overall territorial structure of Balhae is presented in the *Xin Tangshu*, which details the administrative divisions: "The old territory of Sukshin became Sanggyeong (上京, Upper Capital), and its southern part became Junggyeong (中京, Central Capital). The old territory of Yemak became Donggyeong (東京, Eastern Capital), the old territory of Okjeo became Namgyeong (南京, Southern Capital), and the old land of Goryeo became Seogyeong (西京, Western Capital)…The ancient territory of Buyeo was divided into Buyeo-bu and Makhil-bu, and the ancient land of Eupru became Jeongri-bu and Anbyeon-bu. The old area of Solbin became Solbin-bu, the old area of Bulyeol became Dongpyeong-bu, the old area of Cheolli became Cheolli-bu, and the old area of Wolheui became Hoewon-bu and Anwon-bu."

In the process of such extensive territorial expansion, Balhae maintained friendly relations with neighboring countries, exchanging envoys with the Tang dynasty more than 160 times and with Japan about 34 times. Notably, the frequency of interactions during King Mun's reign accounts for one-third of these exchanges, providing insights into the international dynamics of Northeast Asia during this period.

Suryeong, Pioneers of Foreign Negotiations

The *Cefu yuangui* (冊府元龜), which covers the processes of diplomatic negotiations, and the *Shoku Nihongi* (續日本紀), both draw attention to the individuals called suryeong of the Magal peoples. A total of 125 entries can be found in the *Cefu yuangui* about the external activities of these suryeongs related to negotiations with the Bulyeol Malgal, Wolheui Malgal, Cheolli Malgal, Heuksu Malgal, and Uru Magal. These can be further divided into examples such as envoys from Balhae to the Tang, from Malgal tribes to the Tang, and from both Balhae and Malgal tribes to the Tang. The category of the Malgal tribes to the Tang can be further divided into the case of the Malgal tribes sending mission on group basis, and the case of the Malgal tribes sending mission on individual basis.

According to the *Jiu Tangshu*, the first diplomatic exchange between Balhae and the Tang happened in 705, when the Tang "sent a mid-level official, Zhang Xingji, in a reconciliatory effort towards Dae Joyeong, who, in return, sent his son to the Tang court." The *Cefu yuangui* also has an entry for the first year of Emperor Xuanzong's reign (713) stating that "the prince of Malgal paid a visit to the court." From then on, Balhae sent 91 missions of their own to the Tang, while the Malgal tribes sent 22 missions of their own to the Tang dynasty.

The official Balhae missions sent under the tributary relation with the Tang were led by its royal members, whereas in the case of Malgal, the primary negotiators were often *daesuryeongs* (大守令, great chiefs) or *jangguns* (將軍, generals). Just as Balhae sent members of the royal family to lead diplomatic missions after the installation of the king, it may have been natural for the Malgal peoples to involve their leaders in diplomatic activities. The major Malgal tribes that independently negotiated with the Tang were the Bulyeol Malgal, the Cheolli Malgal, and the Wolheui Malgal.

Suryeong, Core of Balhae Economy

Until the first month of 725, when Balhae brought the Heuksu Malgal under control, the Malgal tribes associated with the Heuksu had actively traded with the Tang. From this time on, however, their exchanges with the Tang decreased sharply, only to resume sporadically from the eighth month of 735. What could have been the reason for their disappearance from the foreign negotiation process? The key to unraveling this mystery lies in the suryeong, who were the main actors in foreign negotiations.

History records that not long after Balhae was founded, Balhae "subjugated Buyeo, Okjeo, Joseon, Byeonhan, and several countries north of the sea." During this process, the suryeong figures of Malgal, who were integrated into the central administration of Balhae, expanded their scope of activities in foreign negotiations. It was this class of suryeong rather than the aristocratic class of Balhae who actually carried out foreign trade on a large scale. Domestically, they were chiefs of the Malgal tribes in charge of local rule under Balhae's jurisdiction. Externally, they served as emissaries to the Tang and Japan to engage in trade with those countries; in particular, they traded popular indigenous goods such as sable fur, which was produced widely across the areas covering Buyeo, Eumnu, Eastern Okjeo, and the Bulyeol Malgal. They actively participated in Tang missions as many as 160 times and in missions to Japan 34 times.

11.
King Seon: Enhancing Balhae's Stature as the Haedongseongguk

Kim Eunkuk

Stabilizing the Kingship

When the tenth king Seon (Dae Insu), ascended the throne, Balhae had been established for 120 years. However, in the short span of 25 years between King Mun's death in 793 and Dae Insu's ascension in 818, Balhae went through six successions: the deposed king Dae Woneui, King Seong, King Gang, King Jeong, King Hui, and King Gan. When King Seon, who was from the collateral family line, ascended the throne, royal authority once again waned. These frequent changes in the monarchy have attracted the attention of scholars and prompted a careful analysis of the development of Balhae's history.

The Biography of Balhae in the *Xin Tangshu* describes in some detail several kings' line of descent and their circumstances of death. Such stories tell about the prosperity of Balhae on one hand, as well as the contradictions and crises latent inside the kingdom under King Mun's rule on the other hand. In the end, a prolonged period of internal political turmoil took place immediately after the death of King Mun in 793. As a consequence, the throne was taken not by King Mun's direct descendants, but by his collateral brother Dae Woneui. Yet, right after Dae Woneui's ascension to the throne, a descendent of King Mun killed him with assistance from the country's noble class, and placed one of King Mun's descendants, Dae Hwayeo, on the throne as King Seong. The next year, when King Seong died, King Mun's eldest grandson, Dae Sungrin, succeeded the kingship as King Gang to rule Balhae for the next fifteen years. Following the death of King Gang in 809, his three sons [King Jeong (Dae Wonyu), to King Heui (Dae Eoneui), to King Gan (Dae Myeongchung)] took throne in succession within the short span of less than ten years. The last one, King Gan ruled for only one year. The reasons behind these frequent changes of power have yet to be clearly established, but they must have been closely related to internal political conflicts.

Balhae's Strature as the the Haedongseongguk
(Flourishing Kingdom of the East)

After ascending the throne, King Seon (Dae Insu), sought to increase Balhae's prosperity and actively revive the courageous spirit of the old Goguryeo people. Thus, by "occupying Silla in the south and attacking various regions in the north to establish many prefectures and counties,"[2] as recorded in the Study on Geography 2 of the *Liaoshi* (遼史, History of the Liao), King Seon quickly led Balhae out of adversity and into a powerful position. The phrase "occupying Silla in the south" may suggest a conquest, but such stories do not appear in the historical records. Alternatively, it is plausible that during King Seon's reign, Balhae had become so powerful that Silla did not dare to cause trouble, leading to the stabilization of their respective territories. As for the occupation of various northern regions, this points to the conquest of various regions under Heuksu Malgal. Some researchers include the Cheolli, Wolheui, and Bulyeol regions, but the Heuksu region had already been attacked during the reign of King Mu. Moreover, it was impossible to attack the Heuksu region directly because Cheolli and other regions were located between Balhae and the Heuksu region. It is likely that Balhae had already conquered Cheolli long before the time of King Seon's attack on the Heuksu Malgal, and eventually the local administrations in these regions were established by King Seon.

The Tang readily approved King Seon's enthronement and appointed him to various titles, including *Jianxiao mushujian* (檢校祕書鑒, Inspector-Secretary), and upgraded his honorary appointment to *Jianxiao sikong* (檢校司空, Inspector-Minister) in 820. The Biography of

---

2 南定新羅 北略諸部 開置郡縣

Balhae in the *Xin Tangshu* explains clearly the background of these honorary appointments, stating that "[Dae] Insu conquered many provinces north of the sea and expanded the [Tang] territories, hence his merit deserves the appointment as Inspector-Minster." Thus, the Tang dynasty supported and encouraged Balhae's expansionist policy, which was one crucial factor behind King Seon's successful campaigns. During this time, Balhae and Tang maintained a close relationship. Twenty-four tribute missions were sent from Balhae to the Tang during the twelve years of King Seon's rule, and they received audiences from the Tang Emperors Xianzong, Wuzong, and Wenzong, as well as gifts. Based on his kingdom's internal stability and strength, King Seon also sent six missions to Japan to foster friendly relations. They received the favorable reception and praise of the Japanese Emperors Saga (嵯峨) and Junna (淳和), who remarked that "[King Seon] cultivated trust and courtesy" (*Ruiju kokush*i, 類聚國史, fascicle 194).

In the meantime, Balhae's frequent missions to Japan caused concern on the part of the Japanese. Balhae's envoys, mostly commercial in nature, had a significant impact on the Japanese market, leading some Japanese to refer to them as "merchants rather than neighboring guests,"[3] and stating that the "missions should be stopped from entering the capital"[4] (*Ruiju kokushi*, fascicle 194). Subsequently, Japan requested that the visit number of Balhae missions be limited to once

---

3 實是商旅 不是鄰客

4 停止客徒入京

every twelve years. Despite such restraint, however, King Seon made sure that the gifts from a Japanese Buddhist monk Yeongseon (靈仙), who was studying in the Tang, were safely sent to Japan via Balhae's missions. These efforts were praised by later generations in history as strengthening Sino-Japanese friendship.

According to the Biography of Balhae in the *Xin Tangshu*, Balhae kings from the beginning sent scholars to the Tang capital to study at the Taixue (太學, Imperial College of Supreme Learning) and learn about Chinese institutions, which expedited Balhae's development. By the reign of Dae Hyeonseok (13th king), Balhae firmly attained a high position in international politics and trade, known as the *"Flourishing Kingdom of the East."*

During the reign of King Mun (Dae Heummu), Balhae had already laid the foundation for a prosperous nation through various efforts. Despite some subsequent short-term setbacks, Balhae embarked on a full-fledged path of revival during the reign of King Seon. The reign of the next king, Dae Ijin, was also marked by further development of Balhae, which found its entry in the Biography of Balhae in the *Xin Tangshu*. However, the subsequent history of Balhae was lost and not passed down to future generations.

Between 834 and 835 under the reign of Dae Ijin, Zhang Jianzhang (張建章) of the Tang dynasty was appointed to the post of Adjutant of Yingzhou (瀛州司馬), and dispatched to Balhae as an envoy. While staying in Balhae, he observed features of Balhae's politics and economy, and recorded them in the *Records on Balhae* (渤海記, three fascicles), which were included in the *Xin Tangshu*. These notes have served as a major source of information on Balhae to the present day.

The reign of Dae Ijin saw Balhae's administration divided into five capitals, 15 provinces, and 62 districts, as well as its largest territorial extent. A well-established hierarchical bureaucracy was organized into functional departments and agencies. The military forces were organized into ten guards (wi 衛), with 10,000 men each, and later reinforced with a special unit, and three right and left armies,[5] amounting to a total of 200,000 strong, twice as many as the number of soldiers under the reign of King Mu (Dae Muye). The number of households also increased from 100,000 to 200,000, indicating an expanding base of taxation and military service.

The economy also flourished during this period, with a variety of products being produced and well-received both domestically and internationally. Industries such as hunting and livestock farming continued to grow, while agriculture and various handicrafts had already become major production sectors. The division of labor became more sophisticated by the day, and the variety and quantity of goods continued to expand. In agriculture, crops such as cotton, ramie, pears, and melons were cultivated in addition to rice, wheat, barley, and beans, and both staple and cash crops were widely grown.

---

5   左右神策

Crafts such as weaving, dyeing, ironworking, and copper refining had reached a certain level of development. In trade, active commercial activity emerged, with specialty goods being sent to China or Japan in exchange for needed commodities. Overall, under the reign of King Dae Ijin, Balhae progressed in all areas, leading to the rise of the *"Flourishing Kingdom of the East."*

The reign of the thirteenth King Dae Hyeonseok also achieved stable internal politics and economic development. Notably, the internationally famed poet of Balhae, Bae Jeong (裵頲), reflects Balhae's cultural growth and finesse. It is only natural that Balhae was seen as the *"Flourishing Kingdom of the East."* in the eyes of outsiders.

12.
Universality and Specificity of Balhae's Culture

Kim Eunkuk

History of the *Gonu* Game

For many Koreans, the gonu game has remained a symbol of their childhood, when they would run around on the playground and play various games, including gonu. In the gonu game, the players draw a playing board on the ground and place pieces (or pawns) to play. Although the history of the gonu game is quite old, records explaining its origin are hard to find. It seems to be a rudimentary form of Chinese chess (Kr. janggi 將棋) or Go (Kr. baduk), but it is considered a revised version by Koreans. Gonu was a popular pastime and was the subject of Kim Hongdo's genre paintings in the Joseon era. The rules of the game are so simple that farmers can play it during their break time in the fields, or children can enjoy the game by drawing their boards either on the ground or on paper. There are three ways to win the game:

capture as many of your opponent's pieces or chips (Kr. mal, meaning pawns) as possible, capture your opponent's houses, or checkmate your opponent's pieces. The gonu game varies in name and method from region to region: with names including *kkon, goni, kkoni,* and *kkonu,* and methods encompassing *well gonu* (Kr.umul gonu), *four-line gonu* (Kr. neokjul gonu), *field gonu* (Kr. baat gonu), *pumpkin gonu* (Kr. hobak gonu), *spring gonu* (Kr. Sam gonu), *river gonu* (Kr. gang gonu), *line gonu* (Kr. jul gonu), *number eight gonu* (Kr.palja gonu), *and number ten gonu* (Kr. sipja gonu) in method. As suggested by the variety of its name and methods, the gonu game is very flexible in its way of playing, unlike Chinese chess or Go, which have a formal board and rules.

Types of the Gonu Game

The etymological origin of the term gonu is unknown. In various regions, it is referred to as *kkonu, goni,* and *kkon*. It is also called jigi (地技) in Chinese characters, since it can be played on the ground. Based on the shape of the board, it is also called *well gonu, line gonu, Flower Gonu, and pumpkin gonu,* each of which has slightly different rules of play. In the gomu game, the low-level player makes the first move, and the game will be won by the player who puts the enemy pieces in check or captures as many pieces as possible. The game board on the ground or on paper is called *malpan* in Korean, meaning a running field for horses.

- Well Gonu (River Gonu, Spring Gonu):

In well gonu, players designate a well on the board and place two of their pieces on it. Pieces from either side cannot cross the well. At the start, the player with the restricted pieces moves first. Players take turns, and the first player to block the path of the opponent's piece and prevent it from moving wins.

- Line Gonu (Field Gonu, Straight-line Gonu):

In line gonu, players can create variations such as "four-line gonu" or "five-line gonu" based on the straight lines drawn on the board. Pieces can move in straight lines, either one step or multiple steps, vertically or horizontally. When a player's two pieces are placed on opposite sides of an opponent's piece, that piece is surrounded and captured. The player who successfully encircles and captures all the opponent's pieces wins.

- Gonjil Gonu (Gonji Gonu, Cham Gonu, Line Gonu, Flower Gonu)

The game is played by placing pieces alternately on one of the twenty-four intersections of the board, regardless of direction (horizontal, vertical, diagonal). When three pieces are placed in a row, it is called *gon*. When a gon is reached, the player takes away one of the opponent's pieces, which will put the opponent in a disadvantageous position. Players continue to move their pieces one space at a time in alternate turns, trying to make a gon by aligning three of their pieces in a row. If a player cannot make a gon and has fewer than three pieces left, he or she loses. The game serves as a fun and educational way for children to learn the basics of strategy and tactics, similar to chess and Go. The game, with various board layouts and the option for players to invent new ones, shows diversity in folklore and play.

The Meaning of *Gonu* Culture

There are no detailed guidebooks on the gonu game in Korea, because it was considered a game for lower-status people. Still, the fact that an encyclopedic dictionary of late Joseon, the *Jaemulbo* (才物譜), has an entry for "well gono," and that there is a saying "the first move in the well gonu" figuratively meaning to put the opponent in check, suggests that the gonu game has a long history. Moreover, the Soswae Garden (瀟灑園), which was built more than 100 years ago, has an inscription of gonu on its floor, and a ceramic firing site in Hwanghae-do dated to the early tenth century includes a cham gonu board. These artifacts suggest that the gonu game had been played before the Goryeo dynasty in Korea. Etymologically, the term "well gono" in the *Jaemulbo* is older form of well gonu, and the meaning of gono is to aim at somebody or to stare at somebody, as seen in a sentence in the Korean translation of Zhu Xi's *Elementary Learning*

(小學諺解).⁶ Thus, the term gonu was a derivation from gono, whose meaning of "to aim at or to stare at" was borrowed in designating the game, in which two players aim/stare at each other as opponents.

The gonu game has various rules and boards, yet there are two basic ways to win the game: checkmate the opponent's pieces or chips, as in well gonu and pumpkin gonu, or capture as many of the opponent's pieces as possible, as in line gonu and flower gonu. With its variations, players can choose an appropriate type of the game according to their age. Just like Chinese chess or Go, playing gonu can help in intellectual development. It has become a game enjoyed by many Koreans even today, as it requires thinking about how to move the pieces strategically, fostering deductive and predictive skills.

The Gonu Road and Its Universality

The sites of gonu relics are by no means confined to the Balhae Yeomju (鹽州) Fortress in modern-day Kraskino in the Yeonhaeju. In Mongolia, games such as camel's dig, jirge, and hanungjirge are similar to Balhae's well gonu, gonjul gonu, and palpal gonu. In Mexico and among Native Americans, games such as yutnori, kite flying, spinning tops, jumping games, throwing games, jukmagou (a kind of tug-of-war), hide-and-seek, wrestling, and marbles were played. There

---

6   The original sentence reads: "noppeumyeo natgaom eul 'gono'wa makhida" 높프며 낫가옴을 고노와 막히다.

Chapter 4 ESTABLISHING AUTHORITY 111

Gonu Boards Unearthed from Yeomju Fortress in Kraskino

are even reports of sheaf burning games. In addition, the Jerash archaeological site in Jordan has distinct traces of cham gonu boards, similar to those found along the gonu road around Yeomju Fortress.

We should also pay attention to the small *pieces* uncovered during the excavation of Yeomju Fortress. These pieces make up a significant portion of the artifacts, and they were made for the purpose of playing. In 2004, during the excavation of Yeomju Fortress, gonu boards were discovered, which confirmed that these small pieces were indeed gonu pieces. The recurrent discovery of gonu tiles at Yeomju Fortress in Kraskino, demonstrates the long-standing presence of leisure and diversity in the lifestyle and culture of the Balhae people.

The usefulness of the Sillado (新羅道, Silla Road) between the Southern (i.e., Silla) and Northern Kingdoms can be confirmed by the reassessment of the discovered gonu boards. Following the remains left by the Balhae people leads us to the present-day Mongolian region. Based on a comparison of the Khitans' Chintolgoi Fortress in Mongolia and Balhae's Yeomju Fortress in modern-day Kraskino, it is believed that the relocated Balhae remnants played an important role in spreading their homeland culture to other regions beyond their original territory. Subsequent comparative studies focused on the gonu boards unearthed during the 2004 excavation of Yeomju Fortress tell us that these boards date from before the early 9th century. They are identified as the Korean traditional cham gonu board type, and are found extensively throughout the Korean territory from the Hangpadu-ri historic site on Jeju Island to Gaeseong's Goryeo palace site (Manwoldae), and to Hwanghaenam-do, and even reached Yeomju Fortress across the Duman River. The gonu board discovered at the Goryeo palace site (number 7) in Gaeseong by the joint South and North Korean team in 2007 is 30 centimeters in length and 30 centimeters in width, inscribed on the brick floor of an elegant building. It is dated to the mid-thirteenth century. In addition, the recently discovered gonu board from Jeju Island's Hangpadu-ri is dated to the 13th century, while the gonu boards discovered in Zhongyuan (中原) of China and Xara-balgas in Mongolia are dated to later than the 10th century. Therefore, the gonu boards from Yeomju Fortress in Balhae are among the earliest artifacts from Korea, along with the Silla gonu boards. Reflecting the extensive distribution of gonu games and gonu boards, I came up with the concept of the *Gonu Road*.

The Gonu Road can be a new research topic in the history of the Southern and Northern Kingdoms. In Korean history, the 7th to 10th centuries are considered the era of the Southern and Northern Kingdoms, during which Silla and Balhae developed in the south and north, respectively. However, there was a lack of concrete evidence to support this idea. Therefore, the (cham) gonu board unearthed at Yeomju Fortress must be reevaluated as tangible evidence linking the history of the two kingdoms.

CHAPTER 5
FOREIGN RELATIONSHIPS

13.
Exchanges with Neighboring Countries through Land and Sea

Kim Eunkuk

East Sea as an Exchange Channel between the Southern and Northern Kingdoms

The East Sea(Kr. Donghae 東海, Japan Sea) is a symbol of Koreans and Korean history that opens the national anthem and evokes an image of origin associated with the East. Balhae also has a strong connection with the East Sea, to the extent that it was given the title *Flourishing Kingdom of the East*. However, the role of Balhae in the history of the East Sea has yet to be fully defined. Balhae and Silla in the north and south, respectively, dominated the land and sea, and it is essential to pay close attention to the East Sea as a symbol of their exchange in order to accurately restore the history of the Southern and Northern Kingdoms.

The historical context of referring to Balhae and Silla as the Southern and Northern Kingdoms in Korean history originates from the accounts in the *Samguk sagi* (三國史記, History of the Three Kingdoms) which referred to Balhae as the Northern Kingdom. It is recorded that Balhae sent envoys to Silla twice, during the reigns of King Hyoso and King Sinmun of Silla. In addition, the *Xin Tangshu* (新唐書) describes a route to Silla called the *Silla Road*, which was one of the five routes leading out of Balhae. Balhae established these routes to facilitate its interaction with neighboring countries, but at the same time, they helped the neighboring countries conduct smooth exchanges with Balhae. The Silla Road corresponds to the area centered around the East Sea. This region includes today's northeastern region of China, Yeonhaeju region, and North Korea.

Donggyeong and Namgyeong are believed to be the two points of departure for the East Sea from the Balhae's court. There have been various arguments over where Namgyeong was located, proposals including Hamheung and Baekun Mountain Fortress. In recent years, however, Bukcheong Earthen Fortress has been viewed as the most likely place of Namgyeong. As to the location of Donggyeong, only Bugeo-ri in North Korea has received historical and archaeological attention, but more research and discussions are needed. There is little doubt that both Namgyeong and Donggyeong served as starting points of Balhae's Silla Road that went along the East Sea coast to reach Silla. It is highly probable that in 764 a Chinese envoy, Han Chaocai (韓朝彩), also took this seacoast route established between the Southern and Northern Kingdoms, when he went to Silla via Balhae. That the center of Namgyeong was called *Namhae-bu* (南海府, South Sea province), and the fact that the *Xin Tangshu* calls the Silla Road the *Silla Road of the South Sea* suggest that the Silla Road went along the seacoast of the East Sea to connect Balhae's Southern Capital Namgyeong to Silla.

As to the location of Donggyeong, the archeological evidence supporting Bugeo-ri in North Korea as a possible location is not yet solid, and the site of Pallyeon (Ch. Balian, 八連) Fortress in modern-day Hunchun should be considered alongside Bugeo-ri. It has been widely known that Namgyeong and Donggyeong were fortresses connecting Balhae to the East Sea, through which Balhae had exchanges with Silla to the south and Japan to the east.

Balhae's Foreign Relations

• Relations with the Heuksu Malgal

The Heuksu Magal (Ch. Heishu Mohe) resided in the middle and lower reaches of the Heilong River, and began to expand their power from the Tang era. There was a time when it belonged to Balhae, but mostly it maintained independence. The Heuksu Malgal shared some cultural features with Balhae, but at the same time they formed their own distinct culture. The relations between Balhae and the Heuksu

Malgal varied with the growth and decline of Balhae. In the early years of Balhae, the Heuksu Malgal remained a subordinate entity and maintained friendly relations with Balhae. After the fall of Balhae, however, they evolved into a powerful force known as the Jurchens.

The Heuksu Malgal had managed to maintain their unique characteristics among other Malgal groups, and their level of subordination to Balhae depended largely on Balhae's international stature in the northeastern Asia. King Mu, Balhae's second ruler, adopted the era title of *Inan* (仁安, Benevolent Peace), as soon as he took the throne. Building on the foundations laid down by the founder King Go, he pursued a policy of territorial expansion and elevated the position of Balhae. King Mu's policies inevitably brought about conflict with the Tang dynasty, and in 732, Balhae attacked a Tang city, Dengzhou (登州).

This incident was traditionally interpreted as a simple military clash between Balhae and the Tang. However, Balhae had sufficient grounds to launch an attack against Dengzhou. First, the geographical location of the city played a role. At that time, Dengzhou was an essential logistical point in the maritime trade of East Asia. Therefore, securing the city would have been of great importance to Balhae. Dengzhou also had the Sillagwan (新羅館, Silla Office) and the Balhaegwan (渤海館, Balhae Office) where Silla and Balhae envoys stayed, and Balhae's attack on Dengzhou in 732 can be better understood as an attempt to secure a trade hub between Silla and Balhae. This indicates that Balhae was a maritime empire with warships capable of controlling the seas and merchant ships for maritime trade.

• **Relations with the Turks**

The Turks (突厥) dominated the area centered around the Mongolian steppe for about 200 years from the mid-sixth century. They were divided into the eastern and western empires, and it was the eastern Turks that had significant relations with Goguryeo and Balhae. King Go, the founder of Balhae, wisely took advantage of the geopolitical situation in East Asia and laid a foundation for development, including sending envoys to the Turks when facing threats from the Tang dynasty.

Most notably, King Go defeated the Tang forces that pursued him during his eastward expansion, proclaimed the establishment of Jinguk, and sent envoys to confer with the Turks. These events indicate that the relationship between Balhae and the Turks was highly significant.

Later, the relationship between Balhae and the Turks was influenced by the degree of intimacy between Balhae and the Tang dynasty. Balhae and the Turks became closer after the second king of Balhae, King Mu, launched a surprise attack on the Tang city Dengzhou, but as the Tang improved its relations with Balhae and defeated the Turk forces, Balhae's relations with the Turks were severed.

• **Relations with the Uighurs**

It is well known that Balhae used five major routes - namely, the Amnok Road, Yingzhou Road, Qidan Road, Japan Road, and Silla Road, to actively promote foreign relations with neighboring states. Apart from these five major routes described in the *Tangshu* (唐書), there were other exchange routes, one of which was the Black Sable (黑貂) Road for trading activities.

The discovery of Sogdian silver coins of Central Asian origin in places such as the Novogoreevskoye villages suggests that Balhae actively engaged in trade and economic exchanges with the Central Asian peoples, reflecting its open-door foreign policy. Additionally, the discovery of the Turkic characters and signs of Nestorian Christianity (Kr. Gyeonggyo, 景敎) is also indicative of Balhae's contact and exchange with Central Asian peoples.

• **Relations with the Shiwei**

Balhae also interacted with the Shiwei (室韋). Balhae's initial relations with the Shiwei were friendly, but became tense when the Shiwei aided the Tang by sending their cavalry to the battle of Mt. Madou. The relationship between Balhae and the Shiwei also varied depending on the relationship between Balhae and the Tang. It is known that Balhae had various relationships with entities such as Buyeo, Okjeo, and the Yemaek people.

As seen above, Balhae was a strong maritime and continental

power controlling both the land and the sea. The rulers of Balhae did much to elevate its stature by maintaining active and equal relations with the neighboring states. Thus, the Balhae exchage routes can be understood as the eastern end of the Silk Road.

14.
Popularity of Balhae Products in East Asia

Kim Jinkwang

Balhae remains a mysterious land prompting us to ask many questions. What did the Balhae people eat and wear? What kind of tools did they use in cultivating crops, and what weapons did they use for hunting and warfare? Did they produce rice, which is now a staple food for Koreans? Did they eat soybean paste, a favorite food of Koreans? Did they like to have pork and seafoods? What kinds of products were exchanged between Balhae and the Tang or Japan? What goods did they import? Countless questions cross our minds.

Valuable Local Products for Export

Balhae was a multi-ethnic state. The core forces behind the founding of Balhae were the Goguryeo people who originally lived in the old territory of Goguryeo, and the Malgal people who accompanied them on their escape from Yingzhou. As the country expanded, various tribes that had been scattered by the war of Goguryeo and the Tang were incorporated into the new Balhae. Balhae's vast territory stretched from the Liao River in the west to the East Sea in the east, and from Khabarovsk in the north to the Ni River in the south. This covered a distance of 5,000 *li* in all directions, demonstrating the diversity of the Balhae population as well as the complexity of their economic industries. From mountainous regions as the Mt. Baekdu, the Laoye Range, and the Zhangguangcai Range, to water-drainage regions, such as the Xingkai Lake, the Jingpo Lake, the Liao River, the Amnok River, and the Heilong River, to the coastal region adjoining the East Sea, to the vast plains used for agriculture, and to the flatlands suitable for rice cultivation, Balhae's diverse environments covered the entire territory of this area. The abundant goods produced throughout the country were transported from city to city along major trade routes, both by land and by water, creating a truly impressive sight.

The valuable local products of the country included rabbits of the Mt. Taebaek(Mt. Baekdu) sea kelp from the Namheae-bu, soybean malt from the Chaek-sheng, deer from Buyeo-bu, pig of Makhil, horse of Solbin, hemp from Hyeonju, cotton from Okju, silk from Yongju, iron from the Wi-sheng, rice from the

No-sheng, carp of the Mita Lake, and the Hwando region was known for plum, while the Nakyu region was renowned for pear.

- The Xin Tangshu

Local products of great variety represented their respective locales, and were known for their good quality, abundance, or rarity. There were many specimens of local crops, animals, and handcraft that were unique to certain locales, which came to be known not only within the country but also abroad.

A Variety of Balhae Specialties

At its peak, Balhae's territory included 5 Gyeong (京, capital), 15 Bu (府, Provinces), and 62 Ju (州, county) administratively divided into Gyeong, Bu, Ju, and Hyeon (縣, District). Balhae's local products were produced in all these administrative units beginning with Mt. Taebaek, the birthplace of the Balhae people. Namhae, speculated to be today's Wonsan, was a province of Namgyeong and was known for sea kelp, and the Chaek-sheng (today's Baliancheng, Hunchun City, Jilin-sheng) was famous for soybean malt. In the Buyeo-bu and the Makhil-bu in modern Ningan City, Jilin-sheng, deer and pigs were raised, and the Solbin-bu of Old Solbin Territory produced good horses.

Hyeondeok-bu which is the south of the old Suksin territory was the site of Junggyeong. No-sheng, the first city of Junggyeong, produced rice, and Hyeonju, its second city, was known for hemp. Thus, Junggyeong seems to have been abundantly supplied with food and clothing materials. Yongju, the first city of Sanggyeong of the old Suksin territory was renowned for cloth, and Hwanju of the Seoggyeong of the old Goguryeo territory was famous for plums.

Several quite well-known goods were produced at the county level. The Wi-sheng, a subordinate county of Cheolju of the Hyeondeok-bu in Junggyeong, developed iron industry at its ironsmiths and produced weaponry for soldiers, as well as farm tools for agriculture. Thus, iron scraps produced during the smelting process have been recovered in the Goseong-ri Old Fortress of the Hyeondeok-bu of Junggyeong.

The Mita Lake of Miju of the Anwon-bu was known for carp, and the Dongpyeong-bu in the Old Bulyeol Territory was known for light-emitting gems, sable fur, and white rabbits. It seems that the Anwon-bu had many lakes, and the Dongpyeong-bu of Old Bulyeol Territory was a mountainous coastal region. In sum, Balhae was blessed with its topographical diversity. Therefore, it developed a variety of industries specific to each region, such as rice and beans in the wide field region, sea products in the coastal region, fishing in the lake and stream region, fruits in the hilly region, cloth materials in the forest region, iron smelting and horse raising in the plains region, and animals like deer, rabbits, and sable in the mountainous region.

Sable, Horses, Soybean and More

Balhae's goods were famous not only at home but also abroad. Balhae had about 34 exchanges with Japan and over 160 with China, including visits of the Japanese envoys to Balhae. These envoys returned to Japan with a diverse and valuable array of goods. The most popular of these was sable. The importance of fur in trade with Japan can be seen in the account that the first Balhae's envoy to Japan, Go Jedeok, brought about 300 pieces of sable to Japan.

The popularity of sable was so remarkable that there were even instructions that only high-ranking officials equivalent to the "fourth rank" should wear sable clothing. It is even said that during a sultry and rainy season, the Japanese king attended a banquet wearing eight sets of fur garments made by Balhae. This may have been due to the rarity of high-quality fur production in Japan at that time.

Balhae had far more exchanges with the Tang dynasty than with Japan. Of course, the range of goods exchanged was not as wide as that with Japan, but various Balhae items, including hunting falcons called Haedongcheong, made their way to China. Balhae's good horses (produced in the Solbin region) and refined copper were traded to the Pinglu army, especially after the army moved to the Shandong region in its effort to strengthen its military forces against the Tang.

Balhae's vast land afforded a variety of food materials, so Balhae people enjoyed favorites such as soybean malt, a vegetable called auk in Korean, and garlic. Balhae people were also known for their craftsmanship. Recent archaeological findings have brought to light Balae's three-colored Sancai glazed ceramics, which are comparable to those of the Tang dynasty. Balhae's royal crowns and Buddhist statues were also made using highly sophisticated metalwork techniques. These numerous products of the prosperous era not only enriched the life of Balhae people, but also were transferred to other domestic regions and abroad to the Tang, Japan, and the Turks via the major routes of Balhae.

As illustrated in the records of foreign exchanges, the Balhae people pursued both land and sea routes carrying their valuable goods for trade, indicating their internationally oriented attitude and high spirit of challenge. Dominating East Asia from the 8th to the 10th centuries, the Balhae people had a distinct way of life, including their foods, clothing, activities, transportation, and relationships with neighboring countries. In this brief overview, we have glimpsed how they elevated their country's status in East Asia.

15.
Relations with Japan, as Described in Diplomatic Documents

Kwen Eunju

Importance of Diplomatic Documents

Ancient states in East Asia engaged in various diplomatic activities from an early period. The diplomatic documents that were exchanged were not limited to addressing current issues, but also contained information on the relative status among states and the aspirations of the document-producing state. As a result, they have become important historical materials.

When an envoy with diplomatic documents arrived at the gate of the host country, he first had to declare the purpose of his visit to the local administrative office with documents. The local office would then make a list or copies of the diplomatic documents brought by the envoy and report them to the central authority. After the central authority reviewed and approved the documents, the envoy was allowed to enter the capital and proceed to the central location. Diplomatic documents reflected the hierarchical order among states and were part of the important state protocols of diplomatic etiquette known as *binrye* (賓禮), making them subjects of dispute if not carried or presented in the appropriate formal manner.

The basic diplomatic documents exchanged between Balhae and Japan consisted of two types: the gukseo (國書, state letter) sent in the name of the king, and the cheop (牒, communication letter) exchanged between Balhae and Japan's working-level institutes, the *Jungdaeseong* (中臺省, Central Office) and the *Dajoukan* (太政官, Great Council), respectively. Additional supplementary documents, *byeoljang* (別狀, addenda), were added as needed. The contents of these documents varied and included New Year's greetings, condolences, congratulations on enthronement, communication of international trends, economic trade, military cooperation, and delivery of letters and gifts.

During the time when Balhae and Japan had interests in common, diplomatic documents with an inappropriate format tended to be tolerated, but in times when the interests of Balhae and Japan were in conflict, such small issues could cause disputes.

Strife over the Balhae State Letter

In 727, Balhae initiated diplomatic relations with Japan for the purpose of military assistance or alliance. Previously, in 719, the second king, King Mu, actively pursued a policy of territorial expansion, prompting the pressured Heuksu Malgal to ally with the Tang. In response, King Mu led a punitive expedition against the Heuksu Malgal in 726.

Balhae's expansionist policy also had an impact on Silla. To prepare for Balhae's possible invasion, Silla built fortresses and sought friendship with the Tang dynasty. To counter Silla's moves, Balhae sent envoys to Japan in 727. For a while, there were no major diplomatic disputes between Balhae and Japan, as both shared the goal of containing Silla.

However, as the tensions between Balhae and the Tang dynasty eased and the need to contain Silla diminished, the format of diplomatic documents between Balhae and Japan became a crucial issue in the 750s, marking the beginning of power struggles.

The state letter of King Mu, which was the first diplomatic document sent to Japan, proclaimed his intention to maintain *inho* (隣好, good relations with a neighbor), thus starting the relationship with Japan in the ideal of *gyorin* (交隣, neighborly relations) between the two equal countries. Yet, the letter states that "[Balhae] incorporated and controlled many *beonguk* (蕃國, vassal states) in the vicinity, recovered the old lands of Goguryeo, and continued the customs of Buyeo," thus articulating Balhae's worldview as the successor of the once powerful Goguryeo. This Balhae-centered worldview grew stronger with its growth, and was bound to cause diplomatic conflicts with Japan, as it demanded corresponding recognition on the part of Japan.

From the 750s, Japan also established the centralized *ritsuryō* state system centered on the *Tennō* (天皇, emperor), and wanted to recognize Balhae and Silla as vassal states according to its self-centered worldview. Hence, both Balhae and Japan demanded to each other the diplomatic documents in recognition of the suzerain-vassal relationship. The issue had been latent in time when Balhae and Japan had a mutual interest in checking Silla, yet came to the surface when they lost the common goal. Starting in the 750s, Japan demanded that Balhae write a state letter in the format of *pyomun* (表文), which is a letter from the subject to the emperor. When Balhae did not carry out this request, Japan took issue with Balhae's national ritual as disrespectful. This is known as the State Letter Dispute.

As Balhae established an imperial system from the 770s onward under the third king, King Mun, the state letters expressed its superior position to Japan in the international order by proclaiming Balhae kings as the *cheonson* (天孫, Grandson of Heaven) and by describing the relationship between the two countries as being like that of father-in-law and son-in-law or uncle and nephew, thus provoking discord from the Japanese. Despite the decades-long State Letter Dispute, Japan, unable to assert its position, attempted to impose restirctions on *Binggi* (聘期, the interval between visits) of Balhae envoys.

Japan's Restrictions on the Number of Balhae Embassies, and Prohibition of Private Trade

The term *Binggi* refers to the interval between envoy missions. The first attempt by Japan to impose a Binggi restriction was made in the 790s. Japan limited the visits of Balhae's envoys to once every six years, saying that the sea route for the Balhae envoys was dangerous. However, Japan's intention to limit the intervals of Balhae's envoy missions stemmed from the fact that Balhae had frequently sent large groups of envoys since the 770s, placing considerable economic burdens on Japan. However, this restriction was quickly lifted due to Balhae's demands.

Discussion of the Binggi restriction resurfaced in the 820s. The economic losses caused by Balhae's missions continued to affect both public and private trade in Japan. The items exchanged between the two countries through the envoy missions were all luxury goods consumed by the Japanese ruling class. Since the goods from Balhae were mainly primary products, such as sable, leopard skin, bear pelts, medicinal herbs such as ginseng and honey, and aquatic products, Balhae traders reaped much more profit than their Japanese counterparts.

At the turn of the 9th century, Balhae experienced significant growth to the point of being called *Flourishing Kingdom of the East*. During this time, Balhae pursued diplomacy with Japan primarily for economic reasons rather than political or military ones. Despite the

State Letter Dispute, Balhae's frequent dispatches of large groups of envoys focused on trade, giving the Japanese the impression that Balhae's envoys were not merely *envoys* but rather *merchants*. In addition, internal issues within Japan led to the implementation of the Second Binggi Restriction. In 826, the Second Binggi Restriction was introduced, which was even stricter than the first, limiting envoy missions to once every 12 years. Unlike the first restriction, this one was never lifted. In addition, two years later, Japan prohibited private trade with Balhae envoys.

It was mainly for political reasons that Japan imposed these severe economic sanctions. The State Letter Dispute between Balhae and Japan was related to ceremonial protocols. The protocol for envoys as conducted by traditional East Asian countries reflected the hierarchical status of each country. Balhae and Japan also tried to articulate their international status through the protocol for envoys. Notably, the country that proclaimed itself as an empire held the *Hajeongryeo* (賀正禮, new year's congratulatory reception) every first lunar month, in which foreign envoys were supposed to present the state letter to the emperor as symbolic sign of their belonging to the empire. Thus, the state letter was written in a way that represented the status of the state.

As a result, the two nations engaged in conflicts over the format of the state letters throughout the 8the century and into the 9th century. During this period, Balhae's envoys generally attended Japan's New Year's ceremonies, but they stopped attending around 823. So when

Balhae continued to resist Japan's demands for the format revision of state letters and did not attend the New Year's ceremony, Japan, which had been maintaining diplomatic relations with Balhae despite substantial economic losses, resorted to a more severe stance by implementing the Second Binggi Restriction and banning private trade exchanges. Balhae, discouraged by the loss of trade benefits, suspended its relations with Japan for an unspecified period of time.

The Communication Letters and Economic Diplomacy

Japan's negotiations with Balhae were not only for political purposes, but also to satisfy the consumption needs of Japan's ruling class for foreign goods. However, with the introduction of the 12-year Binggi Restriction and the prohibition of private trade exchanges, Japan's interactions with Balhae's envoys came to a halt. This raised the question of how Japan's ruling class would satisfy its consumer desires. The answer lay with Jang Bogo (張保皐), an influential figure of Silla.

Coincidentally, Jang Bogo was appointed commissioner of the Cheonghaejin (清海鎮) in the same year that the ban on private trade was enforced. In the 830s, Jang Bogo successfully conducted large-scale trade activities with Japan, and it is even said that some Japanese spent fortunes to buy up Jang's goods. However, this situation did not last long. In twelfth month of 841, Balhae's envoys arrived

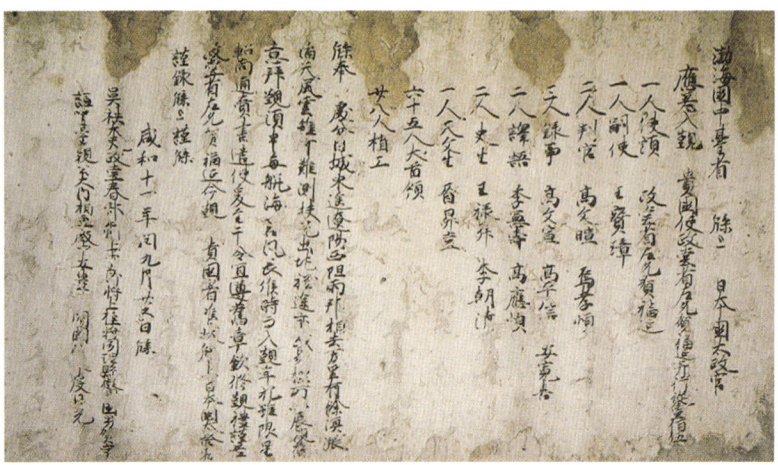

A Copy of Balhae's Jungdaeseong-cheop in 841

in Japan after a long interval, and around the same time, Jang Bogo passed away, leading to the downfall of his maritime forces.

From that point on, Japan was no longer able to secure an official source of foreign trade to replace Balhae. In accordance with changes in the international environment and the economic desires of the ruling classes of both countries, Balhae and Japan sought to make compromises to resolve the ongoing conflicts over diplomatic methods.

Balhae first set the size of the envoy group at 105. This size seemed to be the minimum necessary for Balhae to achieve the desired trade gains while reducing the economic burden on Japan caused by unpredictable large envoy groups. In addition, Balhae avoided New Year's ceremony and Japan no longer took issue with the state letter format.

As the importance of practical contacts overshadowed diplomatic rituals and formalities, the exchange of practical diplomatic documents between Balhae and Japan was meticulously recorded. They are communication letters of the Balhae's Central Office (Jungdaeseong cheop, 中臺省牒) and Japan's Bureau of Great Council (Ja. Daijōkan chō, 太政官牒). The former was to inform the Daijokan in Japan of the names, titles, and numbers of the Balhae envoys. The latter used this information to receive and entertain the Balhae envoys.

In accordance with these changes, not only official trade but also private exchanges regained momentum. In 859, Balhae envoys were allowed to engage in trade with the Heian capital with two marketplaces in the east and west of the capital designated as the venue for their private trade. The Japanese court also officially funded Balhae envoys with 400,000 taels[7] to encourage transactions with the Japanese merchants. Thus, from the mid 9th century onward, Balhae and Japan maintained a unique relationship focused on economic aspects.

---

7 Tael is a weight measure used in ancient China and East Asia. It is a former Chinese monetary unit based on the value of a tael of standard silver.

CHAPTER 6
PEOPLE'S LIVES

16.
Tombs of Princess Jeonghye and Jeonghyo

Kim Jinkwang

The Balhae Princesses Unveiled

In 1949, a breakthrough excavation took place in Mt. Liuding in Dunhua City, Jilin-sheng, China. Breaking the silence of over a thousand years after the fall of Balhae, the tomb of Princess Jeonghye, who was the second daughter of Balhae's third king, King Mun, was revealed to the world. This confirmed that the Mt. Liuding tomb complex was the locale where Balhae's early royalty and aristocracy were buried and affirmed the historical significance of Dunhua as the founding capital of Balhae.

Since then, the Mt. Liuding tomb complex has been excavated several times, where as many as 235 tombs have been found. In general, on the west side of the tomb complex where the tomb of Princess Jeonghye lies, the stone-chambered tombs with earthen mounds are concentrated, while the earthen pit tombs are concentrated on the east side. The Mt. Liuding tomb complex has remained off-limits to the general public. Furthermore, its grave relics, such as the epitaph and the elaborate stone-lion statue, have not been made public. As a result, our understanding of the tomb and its overall appearance relied on photographs in various publications, leaving much to be desired.

In October 2017, the epitaph (tombstone) of Princess Jeonghye, which had excited the academic community studying Balhae at the time of its excavation, was finally revealed at the Museum of Jilin-sheng. The tombstone, originally decorated with vine and cloud motifs, inscribed 725 characters in 21 lines of couplet form written in standard, square style. Originally discovered in seven broken pieces, the epitaph has not been well preserved, and 234 characters on it are illegible. The discovery of Princess Jeonghye, a figure previously unknown through historical records, had significant implications. The inscribed tombstone contained information not only about the princess herself, but also about the ancestors in the royal family, various royal rituals, customs, institutions, and even insights into the royal family's marital life. Although this new information has brought excitement and inspiration among scholars, its remaining illegible part has been a source of disappointment.

This gap in the historical record was alleviated by the 1980 excavation led by Yanbian University at the Mt. Longtou tomb complex, Jilin-sheng, China. A tombstone was unearthed from the tomb of

Princess Jeonghyo, the younger sister of Princess Jeonghye. The tombstone of Princess Jeonghyo, who was recognized as the fourth daughter of King Mun, had an inscription of 728 characters on 18 lines. Compared to the gravestone of Princess Jeonghye, which was found earlier, Princess Jeonghyo's gravestone had a total of three more characters. The contents of the inscriptions were almost identical except for six parts including the identity of the tomb's occupant, the order of the siblings, and details about the children.

Between Happiness and Sorrow

According to the epitaphs of the two princesses, Princess Jeonghye was the second daughter of the third king of Balhae, King Mun, while Princess Jeonghyo was the fourth daughter. Born with the noble aura of the royal family, both princesses were intelligent from an early age and were the envy and admiration of their peers. They received an excellent education and were known for their wisdom. In addition, they both met a match made in heaven and were married. Their happy marital life is epitomized in the epitaphs that "Like a pair of mandarin ducks and noble as phoenixes, they spent beautiful and joyful times together."

Despite their joyful childhood and married life, the two princesses' later lives were not without challenges. Their spouses died suddenly, and to make matters worse, the sons and daughters of the two princesses died young. According to the tombstone inscription, Princess Jeonghye died in 777 at the age of 40. Her son died before reaching the age of taking public office. If the son died before the age of 20, it would suggest that Princess Jeonghye was probably married between the ages of 15 and 20. Of course, if her son died before the age of 15, the time of Princess Jeonghye's marriage would have been later. Expressing the feelings of the time, the inscription reads, "The world is dark everywhere. Nowhere can I see my love, my beloved son. Tears flow endlessly, and the world is filled with ash-colored sorrow.

> You who depart this world for the other world, the path between the mortal world and the afterlife is different. Suddenly, two birds turned against each other and two swords remained separate for good. Before the little child could become a respectable adult, they left this world. And the young daughter, before she could even spin yarn, parted ways.
>
> 所天早化 幽明殊途 雙鸞忽背 兩劍永孤 稚子又夭 未經諸郎之日 稚女又夭 未逢弄瓦之日.

Just as Princess Jeonghye sent her husband and beloved son away at the age of forty, Princess Jeonghyo, her younger sister, passed away at the age of 37, bearing the grief of her beloved daughter's death in 792.

"Grandfather and father established the royal way... shining over the entire world like the sun and moon, upright principles standing firm, and benevolent government covering the world. Their virtues are comparable to those of King Yu of the Xia, being proficient and complete like those of King Tang of the Yin and King Wen of the Zhou.

惟祖惟父 王化所興 … 若乃乘時御辨 明齊日月之照臨 立極握機 仁均乾坤之覆載 配重華而骨夏禹 陶殷湯而韜周文.

Her great ancestors, especially great-great-grandfather King Go (Dae Joyeong), who unified the kingdom, and grandfather King Mu (Dae Muye), who laid the foundation on solid rock, were passed down to her father, King Mun, the Hwangsang. King Mun was praised as comparable to Three Sovereigns and Five Emperors, and to King Wen of the Zhou in his virtues and merits. However, he lost his grandchildren and bid his final farewell to two beloved daughters. He did not hold audiences, abandoned affairs of state, and forsook joyful pastimes and music, only to bid farewell to his deceased daughters with his broken heart and tired body.

The Tomb Relics Showing Balhae's Greatness

The epitaphs of the two princesses provide important information, such as identity of the tomb occupants as the sisters from the same mother, their burial in the ancestral tomb complex, and eulogistic accounts of the Balhae royalty. Other tomb relics such as wall paintings also provide a glimpse into their everyday culture.

The tomb of Princess Jeonghye features horizontal shafts leading to stone tomb chambers, inheriting Goguryeo models and reflecting succession from Goguryeo, while the tomb of Princess Jeonghyo shows a deliberate adoption of Tang practices, particularly in the use of brick for tomb chambers. These changes provide an important understanding of the cultural transformation of Balhae, since the deaths of the two princesses occurred fifteen years apart. It would be worth researching whether these changes represent the Balhae royalty's Sinocentric view or reflect changes in Balhae's inner politics.

The remarkable relics of the two tombs include a stone lion in the tomb of Princess Jeonghye and a wall painting in the tomb of Princess Jeonghyo. The epitaphs on the tombs of the two princesses praised their father King Mun's achievement, who is compared to the status of Three Sovereigns and Five Emperors in light of his long rule of 57 years, during which he made the kingdom strong and rich. This passage provides a glimpse of Balhae's importance in East Asia. During his reign, King Mun used the reign titles of *Daeheung* (大興, Great Rising) and *Boryeok* (寶曆, Valuable Era), ruled the country based on Confucian ideology such as filiality, and spread his virtuous influence among neighboring counties as a Buddhist dharma king. He was called the Sage or Imperial Sovereign, transformed his kingdom into an imperial state, introduced formal institutions for royal families and the crown prince, and built royal tombs.

Treasures of 1,000 Years Old Coming to Light

When I stepped into the Mt. Liuding tomb complex, which was not easily accessible to the public, I had to calm my restless heart, which was beating fast as I looked around. In the Museum of Jilin-sheng, the famous stone lion and the epitaphs of the two princesses, as well as many other relics unearthed, have come to public view. The crouching stone lion of Princess Jeonghye's tomb, featuring sharp teeth in an open mouth, looked as life-like. It was an exciting experience to read directly the real 725-character epitaph written in a standard style, which contained brief account on the princess and her kingdom. In addition, the relics from the Mt. Longtou tomb complex, where the tomb of Princess Jeonghyo is located, include an octagonal silver treasure box decorated with vine and cloud motifs and images of phoenix and wrestler, and a bronze mirror decorated with a variety of animal images on its knob.

The beauty of Balhae culture and art was conveyed in its entirety. As I examined the objects buried with the princesses, I felt their presence and shared the stories they contained, much like sitting down to talk with them, and the affection of the king father toward his deceased daughter princesses.

17.
Three Balhae Men Are a Match for a Tiger

Kim Jinkwang

Manly Balhae Soldiers

The people of Balhae were well-known for their bravery. According to the *Songmo jiwen* (松漠紀聞), recollections by the Song official Hong Hao (洪浩) of his forced sojourn in the Jin territory from 1129 to 1143, Balhae men were said to be "brilliant and courage, surpassing other countries, so that three Balhae men are a match for a tiger." There are many other accounts of the military prowess of the Balhae people. The expansion of Balhae's territory would not have been possible without the outstanding military leadership of Dae Joyeong, renowned for his "courage and skillful military operations," "bringing Buyeo, Okjeo, Byeonhan, Joseon, and other countries north of the sea under his control." Balhae continuously expanded its territory, so a historical record states that Balhae's territory "bordered Silla in the south, encompassed the Wolheui Malgal, and confronted the Heuksu Malgal in the northeast, extending 2,000 *li* on all four directions." This was probably due to the intense military tensions they faced in their confrontations with the Tang dynasty. It could also be a historical legacy from the fall of Goguryeo, which had revered martial arts.

The fierce bravery of Balhae soldiers was symbolized by the names of their military units, such as Maengbunwi (猛賁衛, Fierce Guard), Ungwi (熊衛, Bear Guard), and Biwi (羆衛, Big Bear Guard). An interesting military artifact indicative of military prowess of Balhae men is a Seal of Cheonmun Army (天門軍之印) for celebrating the military feat of the Balhae forces under Dae Joyeong repulsing the pursuing Tang forces at the Cheonmun Pass. It seems that the Cheonmun Army was created to celebrate the military achievements of Dae Joyeong's forces under adverse conditions, despite being inferior to the Tang forces in number.

Playing Gyeokgu as Part of Military Training

The Balhae people always honed their martial skills, often through activities such as gyeokgu (擊毬), a game similar to today's polo. From the statuettes featuring warriors riding horses and hitting balls, along with the depictions of warriors wielding a variety of materials for balls and sticks, it is easy to infer that the Balhae people trained their bodies and learned military tactics through the game of gyeokgu.

There are three extant poems on gyeokgu or tagu (打毬) in Japanese records. One poem titled "Watching Gyeokgu in Early Spring" (早春觀打毬) depicts a scene of gyeokgu played by Balhae envoys in a Japanese courtyard on a spring day, that fascinated the Japanese royalty.

> Filled with the scent of flowers, the morning mist gently lifts as the emissaries appear in the courtyard.
>
> Swinging their sticks through the air, it resembles a crescent moon, as they chase the ball across the courtyard, they look like shooting stars.
>
> First they lean to the left, then they come to the right, jostling near the goalpost. They separate and run, forming a unified mass and emitting a sound like thunder.
>
> Shouting and beating drums, they hasten the outcome, while the spectators can't help but long for all these sights not to be easily accomplished.
>
> - from *Shoku Nihongi* (續日本紀)

This poem was written by Emperor Saga (嵯峨) in 822 when he watched the game played by the Balhae mission headed by Wang Mungu (王文矩). Gyeokgu was a game where players on horseback drove the ball to the opponent's goalpost. It demanded not only individual skills such as horse-riding, ball-driving with a stick, agility, endurance, but also strategic play, unity of movement, and teamwork.

These were elements required for battle, suggesting that this game was probably a form of regular training in Balhae.

Balhae Warriors Equipped with Fine Horses and Iron Weapons

The saying, "Three Balhae men are a match for a tiger," did not only refer to physical strength. As seen in gyeokgu, the core of military power includes not only the martial skills of individual soldiers, but also the corresponding equipment. The mainstay of Balhae's military power consisted of horses, which were the source of mobility, and iron weapons.

Among the well-known products of Balhae were the Solbin horses, bred in the Solbin plateau. Balhae horses were traded to the Pinglu army, especially after the army moved to the Shandong region in an effort to strengthen its military forces against the Tang. The Biography of Yi Jeonggi (Ch. Li Zhengji) in the *Xin Tangshu* states that fine horses from Balhae continued to come into the Pinglu Zhiqing military district. This means that Yi Jeonggi needed the fine breed of Balhae horses to enhance the combat power of his armies against the Tang forces.

Iron weapons were another source of Balhae's combat power. The level of ironworking technology of Balhae can be inferred from historical records and unearthed artifacts. Numerous iron products have been found at archaeological sites and tombs in the areas of the original capital (modern Dunhua), Junggyeong, and Sanggyeong. The *Xin*

Tangshu lists quality iron as one of the representative local products of Balhae, which was produced from Wi-sheng of the Hyeondeok-bu and from Gwangju of the Cheolli-bu. A record says that the Khitans moved Balhae's iron smelteries to their territory after they founded the Liao, suggesting that Balhae people were skilled in producing quality iron. Thus, Balhae warriors could arm themselves with sharp iron weapons and solid helmets.

Brave Military Challenge against the Tang

Balhae men were famous for their bravery, as exemplified in the victorious battle at the Tianmen Pass and the subjugation of the Heuksu Malgal. Their bravery was best exemplified by the military challenge against the much superior Tang. As described in the historical records by a Balhae official, "At the height of Goguryeo's prosperity, its army numbered about 300,000, but it was quickly overwhelmed by the Tang forces. Now our armies are much smaller in number than Goguryeo," and "the Tang have much larger population and strong armies overwhelmingly superior to ours," there was a significant disparity between Balhae and the Tang dynasty in terms of military and economic power.

However, just five to six years after this remark, the Balhae naval forces led by Jang Munhyu (張文休) set out from the mouth of the Amnok (Ch. Yalu) in 732, crossed the sea via the Lushun Bay, and made a surprise attack on Dengzhou (modern-day Penglai in Shandong), an international gateway to the Tang. They succeeded in defeating the Tang contingent of 1,000 strong under the Dengzhou intendent Wei Jun (韋俊). Afterwards, Balhae launched another attack against the Tang at Mt. Madou (near modern-day Qinhuangdao in Hebei), much further into the Tang's interior territory than Yingzhou where Dae Joyeong had set out to found his kingdom against the Tang. Hence, Balhae risked an attack from two sides of Youzhou (modern-day Beijing) and Yingzhou. This hardline policy of Balhae may have been possible because the Balhae forces made an alliance with the Khitans and the Xi, who were active around there.

> The vendetta between Dae Muye (King Mu) and his brother Dae Munye resulted in the latter's exile to the Tang. The imperial edict ordered Kim Saran (金思蘭) to raise the Panyang and Silla armies of 100,000 strong to attack Balhae. Dae Muye sent assassins to Luoyang to kill Dae Munye. The Balhae forces reached Mt. Madou and annihilated the fortresses and towns. Wu Chengci (烏承玭) blocked the main routes and built up the defense stone wall of some 400 *li* to fend off the Balhae forces.
>
> Biography of Wu Chngci in the Xin Tangshu

The Tang's response to Jang Munhyu's attack shows that it was not just a surprise attack. The fact that they mobilized a punitive force of

100,000 soldiers and constructed a barrier of about 400 *li* (about 209 kilometers) to counter Balhae's attack shows the intensity of the situation. This underscores not only the extensive reach of Balhae's cavalry, but also the considerable strength of their offensive capabilities.

Balhae's Military Prowess

The attacks on Dengzhou and the victory at Mt. Madou cannot be viewed without acknowledging the military superiority of the Balhae army. In particular, the landing at Dengzhou relied on ground forces rather than naval power, and this strategy was possible due to their training regimen that involved advanced equipment. Moreover, the surprise attack on Dengzhou was carried into prolonged battles in Shandong and then the Shanhai Pass. All these military capabilities demonstrat that Balhae's military prowess can be attributed to the mass production of good horses, which was a core aspect of mobility, the possession of advanced equipment facilitated by superior iron-working technology, strategic insight into the overall situation and tactics, and the enduring physical strength and cooperative spirit developed through constant training.

Eventually, Balhae men, who inherited the military tradition of Goguryeo, gained the reputation that "Three Balhae men are a match for a tiger," and "Balhae men are brilliant, surpassing other nations in courage." Yang Seongji (penname Nuljae) in the King Sejo era of Joseon asked, "Why did Balhae, which existed for only a few hundred years, earn the title of the *Flourishing Kingdom of the East* rather than the thousand-year history of Silla? The answer probably lies in the great achievements of the Balhae people.

18.
Pastime

Kim Eunkuk

Since its founding, Balhae gradually developed its state institutions and systems of administration and military affairs. Within this framework, the people of Balhae also enjoyed a variety of cultural practices. The focus here is on their culture of entertainment.

Building on the cultural foundations of earlier Goguryeo phases, Balhae assimilated the cultures of neighboring peoples to create a distinctive culture of its own. Its territorial control extended even further than that of Goguryeo, encompassing what is now Yeonhaeju. As a result, the Balhae relics in Yeonhaeju offer a glimpse of both the Goguryeo legacy and the diverse culture that emerged in Balhae.

Sports with Horses

Among the games of the Balhae people, one can first find Chukguk (蹴鞠) and gyeokgu (擊毬). Gyeokgu originated in the Persian region and was transmitted through Tibet, India, Tang, Goguryeo, and Silla. It flourished in Balhae and Silla, as well as during the Goryeo and Joseon periods. The modern game of polo also has its origins in gyeokgu.

Records of Balhae's gyeokgu can be found in Yu Deukgong's *Balhaego* (渤海考). It says that in 889 a group of envoys led by Balhae's Wang Mungu (王文矩) played a game of gyeokgu in Japan before the Japanese king. This indicates the popularity of gyeokgu in Balhae at that time and its direct influence on spreading the game to Japan.

Chukguk was also an ancient game carried over from before Goguryeo, in which a ball made of animal bladder was filled with air and kicked around. It was a common form of entertainment culture.

Like Goguryeo warriors, Balhae men were skilled in archery and horseback riding. The Balhae culture of archery on horseback spread to various regions through intermediaries such as hunting falcons and dogs, good horses, and high-quality bows. Balhae's hunting falcon, known as Haedongcheong (海東青) was a valuable gift in Balhae's diplomatic contacts with neighboring countries. The Solbin (率賓) horses bred in modern Ussuriysk in Yeonhaeju were one of Balhae's special products and were known as the best breed in Northeast Asia. These factors contributed to the strengthening of various Balhae pastimes such as horseback riding, archery, and gyeokgu.

The Yeomju Fortress of Balhae located in modern-day Kraskino in Yeonhaeju is a representative Balhae site with neatly divided streets. Along these streets, artifacts have been discovered that reveal the daily life of the Balhae people. Among them are stones of the gonu game, a traditional Korean game that is found in various forms in the southern, central and northern parts of the Korean Peninsula, including Jeju Island.

Gonu Game

In East Asian history, Balhae's strength continued to shine even after the royal line of the the last king, Dae Inseon (大諲譔), was severed by the surprise attack of the Khitans in 926. The Khitans forcibly resettled the Balhae royal family, nobles, and various segments of the Balhae population for their governance, and the Balhae people continued to play a prominent role in the subsequent Jin and Yuan nomadic states.

Beginning in the 10th century, after the fall of Balhae, the Mongolian steppe came under the rule of various nomadic groups such as the Uighurs and Khitans. During this period, the Khitans transferred descendants of the Balhae people to their inner territory. The Balhae traces in the western part of modern Mongolia could be traced archaeologically through survey and excavation by teams of Korean and Mongolian scholars some twenty years after the two countries established diplomatic relations in the 1990s.

Since then, the archaeological expedition teams of the two countries have continued to conduct excavations at the Balhae sites in Mongolia and in Kraskino in Yeonhaeju. As the Russian scholars who had been part of the expedition to the Kraskino site joined the Balhae sites in Mongolia, they began to identify commonalities between the two sites and their artifacts. The result of this collaboration led to the recognition of a common gonu culture based on the common presence of gonu stones found in both areas. The key discovery in the Korean-Mongolian project was made during the excavation of the Khitan capital in Mongolia. Through an analysis of artifacts, especially the game stones, recovered from the Khitan capital and Yeomju Fortress, it was concluded that the game stones from both places were gonu pieces.

Based on the archaeological analysis and comparison of the findings of gonu pieces and boards from the Korean peninsula, China, and Mongolia, and those from the Balhae site in Kraskino, the concept of the Balhae *Gonu Road* can be suggested as a term reflecting the cultural linkage that connected the Northern (i.e., Balhae) and Southern (i.e., Silla) Kingdoms during the 7th to 10th centuries of Korean history.

Balhae's gonu board and pieces can be seen as a cultural medium in its contact and exchange with its neighboring countries, and their distribution among the Northeast Asian countries. By comparing the Khitans' Chintolgoi Fortress in Mongolia and Balhae's Yeomju

Fortress in Kraskino, we can infer that the relocated Balhae people played an important role in spreading their homeland culture to other regions. A subsequent study focused on the gonu board discovered at the Yeomju Fortress in Kraskino in 2004, which is dated prior to the early 9th century.

Further analysis of the area surrounding Yeomju Fortress revealed that these gonu board were also Korea's traditional cham gonu board, which are widely distributed from Jeju Island to Gaeseong's Goryeo site and to Hwanghaenam-do, and beyond the Duman River to the Yeomju Fortress in Kraskino in Yeonhaeju. The Balhae Kraskino gonu board is said to be the oldest of its kind, along with that of Silla. The recently discovered gonu board from Jeju Island's Hangpadu-ri is dated to the 13th century, while the gonu boards discovered in the Zhongyuan (中原) of China, and Xara-balgas in Mongolia are dated to later than the 10th century.

19.
Clothing Styles and Textiles

Kwen Eunju

Diverse Clothing Styles

Balhae's clothing culture was different from that of the previous Three Kingdoms period (A time when Goguryeo, Baekje, and Silla co-existed). During the Three Kingdoms period, distinctive Korean clothing culture was established. Despite the influence of neighboring cultures, traditional clothing remained dominant. However, after the fall of Goguryeo, a significant portion of Balhae's founding power lived in Tang-controlled Yingzhou (營州, present-day Zhaoyang) for an extended period of time, where they were likely influenced by Tang clothing culture.

During this time, Tang clothing was in vogue in East Asian countries. Balhae's third ruler, King Mun, actively adopted Tang culture. It seems that the royal family and aristocratic society dressed similarly to Tang during this period. The commoners, however, probably retained their indigenous clothing culture, including traditional Goguryeo dress and Malgal clothing. In addition, Balhae had residents of the Khitan, Shiwei, and Turkic backgrounds, who contributed to the coexistence of diverse clothing cultures.

System of Official Attire and Male Garments

Official attire was the clothing worn at formal events and administrative functions in the country. Official attire tended to be introduced at times when royal authority was consolidated and institutional systems were well established.

In the early stages of a nation's establishment, it may have been difficult to implement a well-structured system of official attire. This may have led to the imitation of Goguryeo's ceremonial robes in early Balhae, much like King Wang Geon adopted the administrative practices and dress of Silla in the early days of the Goryeo dynasty. In the mural painting in the tomb of the Tang crown prince Li Xian (李賢), which portrays an envoy ceremony (禮賓圖), an envoy figure with feathers in his headdress is speculated to represent either a Goguryeo or a Silla person. Li Xian died in 684, but his tomb was built in 706. Therefore, there is also an argument that the figure may represent an envoy from Jinguk during the early days of Balhae.

Later, during the reign of the third ruler of Balhae, King Mun, an independent system of official attire seemed to be established as the ruling regime was renewed. The formal attire included the *Bokdu* (幞頭, a type of headdress) and the *Danryeong* (團領, a type of official robe). In the Biography of Balhae chapter of the *Xin Tangshu*, the ranks of officials were divided by *Jil* (秩). It also mentioned that there were four colors for official robes: purple, blue-green, light blue-green, and green. Officials of the top five ranks carried *Hol* (笏) (wooden tablets used to greet royalty) and *Eodae* (魚袋) (fish pouches to indicate rank).

Balhae's Official Attire (Biography of Balhae in the *Xin Tangshu*)

Jil	1	2	3	4	5	6	7	8
Color	Purple			Blue-green		Light Blue-green		Green
Hol	Ivory Hol					Wooden Hol		
Eodae	Gold fish			Silver fish				

We can see Balhae's official attire on the figures in the wall painting of Princess Jeonghyo's tomb. Guards, musicians, and courtiers are shown wearing *Malaek* (red hemp headgear, 抹額) and *Bokdu*. These men wore *Danryeong* as official attire similar to that worn by civilian and military officials. However, military officials wore shorter jackets with narrower bottoms probably to allow freer movement. Men wore belts with their official attire. There were two types of belts worn by Balhae men: *Gwadae* (decorated belt, 銙帶) and *Hyeokdae* (leather belt, 革帶).

There were two kinds of shoes: *Hwa* (靴) and low-necked *Ri* (履).

[Left] Balhae's Hwa (from the Balhae Tomb Mural in Geumseong-ri, Hamgyeongbuk-do, North Korea)
[Right] Ri of Three Kingdoms Period (from the Dalseong Park in Daegu, South Korea)

Attire of the Malgal People (Exhibited in the Museum of Liaoning-sheng)

According to the *Bohai guozi changbian* (渤海國志長編), "the people of Balhae are skilled at making Hwa." They also had high-quality leather shoes called *Ammohwa* (暗摸靴), which made no noise when walking at night. Ri shoes were low-cut shoes that expose the top of

Long-haired Goguryeo Men
(Left: from the Tomb of the Dancers, Center and Right: Changchuan Tomb No.1)

the foot, similar to Koean straw shoes. This type of shoe has been popular in Korea since ancient times.

The clothing of ordinary men at that time cannot be confirmed. It is likely that they wore clothes similar to the traditional Goguryeo clothes in their daily lives. Recently, two stone figures (石用) from the Tang dynasty were unearthed in Chaoyang (朝陽) in Liaoning-sheng, China. Many Goguryeo and Malgal people were brought to this region after the fall of Goguryeo. The shape and style of clothings these stone figures wore are different from those of the Tang or the Khitans. Chinese scholars speculate that these were used by the Malgal people who lived in this region.

However, the descendants of the Malgal people, such as the Jurchens and the Manchus had the Chinese queue hairstyle. Their front of the head was shaved, leaving the hair flowing from the crown to the shoulders. Sometimes the hair was decorated with colorful thread, golden ring, or jade. The stone figures, on the other hand, do not have a shaved head, and their hair falls down their backs.

If we consider the hairstyle in which the hair is pulled back and let fall as in the Chinese queue, we can also find a similar style among the Goguryeo people. For example, depictions of a horseman and a hawk-hunter in the Goguryeo mural at Changchuan Tomb No.1, and a dancer in the Tomb of the Dancers show a similar hairstyle. In addition, the male stone figure holds a haedongcheong, which was a representative falcon of the Korean Peninsula and the Manchurian region. The depiction of another figure holding gwa is also reminiscent of the procession seen in the mural of Princess Jeonghyo's tomb in Balhae. Therefore, these stone figures may represent either Goguryeo or Balhae people.

Female Garments

Artifacts that give us a glimpse of Balhae women's attire include the bronze female statue found in Yeonhaeju, the tri-colored female figure found near Mt. Longtou in China's Jilin-sheng, and the bronze mounted female statue. The bronze female figure wears a wide-sleeved top (大袖袍) with a shawl (雲肩), a long skirt (裳), and a double-bun hairstyle (雙髻). The tri-colored female figure wears an outfit with a long skirt that extends from just above the chest of a long-sleeved top. This attire was common for women during the Tang

Balhae Women's Clothing
(Left: Double-bun Hairstyle Woman, Center: Sancai woman, Right: Bronze Mounted Woman)

dynasty in China and seems to have been popular in Balhae as well. Both female figures wear shoes with a high front, called *Goduri* (高頭履), to prevent the long front apron from getting caught in their feet. The bronze mounted woman also wears a similar garment.

In 2008, pottery from the Balhae period was unearthed in the Koksharovka site in Yeonhaeju. It depicts dancing women reminiscent of *ganggangsullae*, a traditional Korean dance. These women wear tops with narrow sleeves and skirts that fall just below the knees. This attire was probably worn by women of lower social status. It is especially associated with the clothing of the Turks who were incorporated into Balhae.

Dancing Women (from the Koksharovka Site, Yeonhaeju)

Handicraft Textiles

Balhae excelled in textile craftsmanship, producing various types of fabrics, including hemp, ramie, silk, and wool. The Biography of Balhae chapter in the *Xin Tangshu* mentions hemp as a specialty of Hyeonju (顯州). A variety of hemp was produced in Balhae in such large quantities that even after the fall of Balhae, the Khitans collected 100,000 *pil* (bolts) of raw hemp and 50,000 pil of fine hemp annually from the Balhae region. Cotton was mainly produced in Okju (沃州), of Namgyeong Namhae-bu and near present-day Hamgyeong-do in North Korea. Since cotton was in great demand, it was sometimes imported from Japan.

The nobility wore mostly silk clothes. The finest silk was produced in Yongju (龍州) of Sanggyeong Yongcheon-bu. Since the top ruling class of Balhae was concentrated in this area, the highest-quality silk was produced there. Recently, more than 40 types of silk fabrics in a reliquary box have emerged from the sarira casecasket discovered at the Balhae site.

Among Balhae's main exports, leather and fur products were very popular because of their excellent quality. According to records, when Balhae's envoy Bae Gu attended a banquet in Japan, the Japanese prince Shigeakira (重明親王) appeared in eight layers of black sable imported from Balhae, even though it was midsummer, which astonished Bae Gu.

Balhae had an advanced handcraft textile industry and trade relations with neighboring countries with a wide variety of fabrics. This facilitated the creation of various clothing styles and laid the foundation for the development of Balhae's clothing culture.

20.
Letters and Literary Culture

Kwen Eunju

Cultural Foundation of the *Flourishing Kingdom of the East*

Since Balhae was founded in 698, unlike its predecessors such as Baekje, Goguryeo, and Silla, Balhae already acquired knowledge of Chinese characters from the very beginning. Therefore, Chinese records mention that Balhae had "written characters and scribes" (*Jiu Tangshu*) and that they "understood the official documents" (*Xin Tangshu*). In the sixth month of 738, Balhae sent envoys to the Tang dynasty to acquire Chinese literature, and the Dharani Sutra that Balhae transmitted to Japan has been preserved to this day. There was a central institution called *Munjeokwon* (文籍院), which was responsible for organizing and managing documents, and *Jujagam* (胄子監), a national educational institution that systematically cultivated talents. Furthermore, the inscription on the monument erected at the educational institution reads, "Confucian scholars (儒生) swarm in the East Hall (東觀)."

In addition, there were officials known as *Jogosayin* (詔誥舍人) who were responsible for drafting the king's orders. They belonged to the *Jungdaeseong* (中臺省, Central Office). Among the envoys sent abroad were the *noksa* (錄事), who handled documents and other administrative tasks. Diplomatic documents exchanged with neighboring countries indicate that Balhae had developed a systematic document management system.

A number of literary relics from Balhae have been discovered, including the epitaphs of princesses Jeonghye and Jeonghyo, a literary note from the Gaesim Buddhist Temple (開心寺), an inscription on the Yeonggwang Pagoda, and a variety of notes inscribed on porcelain, iron tools, seals, bronze mirrors, bronze plaques, and Buddhist statues. Recently, the tombstones of two Balhae empress have been discovered, but they have not yet been made public by China. In addition, numerous inscriptions on roof tiles and ceramics have been discovered, indicating the development of a rich literary culture in Balhae.

After its founding, Balhae developed rapidly and aspired to an imperial system starting in the reign of its third monarch, King Mun. He established a centralized system with Three Departments and Six Ministries(三省六部) at its core. In order to efficiently govern Balhae's vast territory, an administrative document system was developed, which further promoted culture of writing. It is said that the progress of literary culture coincides with the development of its culture and civilization. Therefore, the advancement of its literary culture can be seen as the foundation of its cultural development, which led it to become the *Flourishing Kingdom of the East* in the 9th century.

Possibility of Balhae's Own Letters

When it comes to literacy in Balhae, however, many people are curious about whether the Balhae people had their own unique script. In the early 12th century, in the Japanese collection of myths and stories called *Kōdancho* (江談抄), there is a story about the characters created by Balhae. In the Engi (延喜) era (901-922), two Balhae envoys presented the communication letter bearing their names written in characters that had been unknown to the Japanese. Although it was written in strange characters, a Japanese man, Kike (紀家), was able to render the "石" and "木" as "ノツフリ丸" and "石ノマフリ丸," respectively, which fascinated people.

Balhae's invention of its own versions of Chinese characters was also known to the Tang. In the *Complete Works of Li Taibai* (李太白全集), specifically in the section of *Yuchen Congtan* (玉塵叢談), there is a story about a letter sent by Balhae to the Tang dynasty that no one in the Tang court could decipher. However, Li Taibai managed to decipher it and replied. The story of Li Taibai deciphering Balhae's characters is also mentioned in the Ming dynasty works, *Gujin qiguan* (古今奇觀) and *Sui Tang yanyi* (隋唐演義). In the stories, Balhae characters are said to resemble birds' foot-prints.

These myths and stories have sparked interest in whether Balhae actually had its own writing system. Recently, many characters engraved on roof tiles have been found at Balhae archaeological sites. Some of them are different from the traditional Chinese characters, further raising the possibility of Balhae's own writing system.

While there are certainly unique characters in Balhae script materials, 80-90% of them are not significantly different from existing Chinese characters. The majority of the remaining characters can be identified as simplified forms, variant forms of Chinese characters. Therefore, based only on the discovered Balhae letters, it would be premature to conclude that the Balhae people created their own writing system in the same way that the Khitan or Jurchen people developed and used an independent script.

Although Balhae's official script was Chinese, it is believed that the language of Goguryeo was used as the official language. In 739, when the Balhae envoy Lee Jinmong and his party attended a royal audience in Japan, a Silla translator was most likely present for the purpose of translation. It shows that the Balhae envoy and the Silla translator could communicate with each other. In this way, Balhae employed the Goguryeo language, which was compatible with the Silla language, and its script probably followed the traditions of

Rubbings of Letter Inscriptions on Balhae Roof Tiles

Goguryeo.

Since Chinese is linguistically distinct from Korean, it was necessary to adapt Chinese characters to the linguistic structure of Korean in the Three Kingdoms period. A notable example is the *Idu* (吏讀) system of Silla, which was influenced by Goguryeo. Balhae probably followed a similar path. In fact, our ancient ancestors even created new Chinese characters. Among the Balhae script materials, newly created Chinese characters may have been created by Goguryeo or by the Balhae themselves. This process is similar to the late Joseon dynasty's creation of the character "乭" (Kr. dol) for the name of the famous anti-Japanese uprising leader, General Shin Dol-seok, in order to write his name in Chinese characters.

Development of Literacy and Diplomacy by Scholars

The tombstones of Princess Jeonghye and Princess Jeonghyo show the level of literacy in Balhae in the 8th century. These tombstones refer extensively to Chinese Confucian classics and historical texts, skillfully employing the parallel-prose (骈儷) literary style of the contemporary Tang. This demonstrates the establishment of literary and scholarly activities during the reign of King Mun. However, the tombs of the two princesses have almost identical contents and contain inaccurately quoted passages.

By the 9th century, Balhae's level of literacy had reached an impressive standard, drawing admiration even from the Tang dynasty and Japan. Balhae sent exceptional scholars and literati as envoys, demonstrating its cultural sophistication. This is especially evident in its diplomatic interactions with Japan.

In the early stages of Balhae, diplomatic relations with Japan were established primarily for military purposes, which led to the dispatch of mainly military officials to Japan. Around the middle of the 8th century, however, more civil officials began to be included among these envoys. As the 9th century progressed, the trend of sending scholars became more pronounced. Notable figures such as Wang Hyoryeong (王孝廉), Go Gyeongsu (高景秀), Seok Injeong (釋仁貞), Ju Wonbaek (周元伯), Yang Seonggyu (楊成規), Lee Heungseong (李興晟), Bae Jeong (裵頲), and Bae Gu (裵璆) were among the Balhae envoys to Japan who also held positions as scholars in Balhae.

In Japan, great attention was paid to the reception of these Balhae scholars. People who were knowledgeable about literature were specially selected to receive the Balhae envoys. For example, it is recorded that Miyako Kotomichi (都言道) even changed his name, believing that his original

Princess Jeonghye Tombstone

name was not suitable for receiving Balhae envoys. When Bae Jeong, known to be a literary genius who could "produce poems in seven steps (七步之才)", went as an envoy, an incident occurred in which Fujiwara Yoshitsugu (藤原良積), who lacked literary skills, felt ashamed and left the gathering during a banquet.

Literary diplomacy reflected the high level of cultural maturity of Balhae society as it entered the 9th century. Through this development, Balhae earned the title of *Flourishing Kindgom of the East*, and the Tang dynasty literary figure Wen Tingyun (溫庭筠) praised Balhae as having "established itself as an equal to the Tang in literary and cultural affairs." This literary tradition was even passed down to the descendants of Balhae, many of whom distinguished themselves in the eras of the Yao (遼)·and the Jin (金).

21.
Housing with Ondol

Kwen Eunju

Housing Culture by Social Status and Geographic Region

Today's modern homes vary in structure and size based on the tastes and preferences of their owners. In the distant past, though, owning a home had more to do with one's ability to afford it, or one's economic status, than with personal taste. This economic capacity was often supported by one's social status.

Similarly, in Balhae, the type of dwelling varied according to the social status and economic level of the owner. With its vast territory stretching thousands of *li* in all directions, Balhae also showed differences in housing culture based on the lifestyle and climate of the regional inhabitants.

Houses can be broadly categorized as above-ground houses and pit houses. Above-ground houses were a more advanced form than pit

House-Shaped Ceramic of Gaya
(Courtesy of Kyungpook National University Museum)

houses and appeared in Korean history after the Bronze Age as heating and architectural technologies advanced. During the Balhae period, the royal family and the nobility, who had high status and economic means, lived in spacious and lavish houses with elevated platforms on which they built houses covered with roof tiles. Commoners also lived in ground-level houses, but they were smaller thatched houses.

Pit houses date back to prehistoric times. Prehistoric people in Manchuria and the Korean Peninsula built pit houses to minimize exposure to the cold by digging the ground and reducing the surface area exposed above ground. As a result, pit houses became deeper the farther north one went. During the Balhae period, although the prevalence of above-ground houses increased, many people still lived in pit houses, especially in impoverished and colder regions. Pit houses can even be found in the living quarters of mountain fortresses.

In Balhae, there are unique remnants of buildings known as "24-stone relics" that show an elevated style (Kr. Gosangsik, 高床式). These structures are similar to Goguryeo's bugyeong (桴京, granaries)

24-Stone Relics (Jiangdong, Dunhua City, Jilin-sheng, China)

and Gaya's house-shaped ceramics, but the "24-stone relic" buildings are considered to have special functions, rather than being just food storage facilities, due to their larger size and the presence of tiled roofs. They are often found at major transportation hubs or crossroads, and are speculated to have transportation-related functions. Other elevated structures were used primarily as ancillary structures to houses, similar to Goguryeo's granaries, rather than as everyday living spaces.

Remains of Balhae Hypocaust at the Western Residence Site in Sanggyeong
(Source: The Illustrated Book of Ruins and Relics of Korea)

Houses of Royalty and Aristocrats with Water Channels and Roof Tiles

Among the remains of houses in Balhae, there are places associated with people of high social status. These include the palace grounds at Yongcheon-bu in Sanggyeong and the remains of houses at Yongwon-bu fortress in Donggyeong, Bukcheong Earth Fortress, and present-day Shuaiwanzi. Although there were differences in size and decoration within the ruling class, their residences were much larger and more splendid than those of the commoners.

The western side of the palace at Yongcheon-bu in Sanggyeong, a prominent residence of the royal family, has a linear arrangement of three rooms with cornerstones and pillars on raised rectangular platforms. It also has outbuildings around the rooms, probably created to cope with temperatures that could drop to minus 20 to minus 30 degrees Celsius in winter. The roof is decorated with exquisite tiles, and a moat surrounds the raised platform. The house faces south. Ondol, a Korean underfloor heating system, is installed in the rooms and parts of the outbuildings. The ondol system has a long "L" shape, with hypocausts running through only part of the room.

The houses of the nobility are smaller than those of the royal family, but have a similar structure. They consist of three rooms facing south, placed on a raised platform with cornerstones and pillars, and equipped with the ondol heating. The platform is surrounded by a moat and the roof is also tiled. There are also houses with stone walls such as the house site discovered at the Shuaiwanzi ruins of present-day Hunchun in China.

The walls of the rooms were often covered with fine clay or lime and decorated with patterns of red and other colors. In cases where the elevated platform was high and substantial, stairs were installed. Several sets of stairs can be seen in the royal living quarters.

Houses of Common People

The common people lived in above-ground houses without elevated platforms, mainly in one-room thatched houses. Some also lived in semi-pit houses. Archaeological remains of villages consisting of semi-pit houses have been found, and the remains of the Bohai (Balhae) village in present-day Tuanjie in Dongning, China are a representative example. The houses in this village are generally rectangular semi-pit structures with an area of about 15-20 square meters. They have a door and a set of earthen stairs leading to the outside.

What stands out in these pit houses, however, is the presence of ondol heating systems, which were not commonly found in pit houses before Balhae. These ondol structures were built of round and flat stones, either stacked or placed directly on the ground, and like the ondol of the noble residences, they also featured the L-shaped corner heating system that ran through part of the room. This archaeological site is considered to be a village of the Malgal people under the rule of Balhae.

In addition to Balhae artifacts, Goguryeo-style clay pots were also discovered at this site. This suggests that the Malgal people, who were under the influence of Goguryeo culture before the establishment of Balhae, adopted the ondol underfloor heating system.

Balhae's *Ondol*, More Developed than Goguryeo

It's clear from the remains of their houses that the Balhae people were particularly fond of ondol heating systems. Balhae's ondol heating systems evolved from and built upon the Goguryeo tradition. While Goguryeo's ondol system often had a single or partial duct design, Balhae's ondol system often had two or even three ducts, expanding the area and increasing heating efficiency compared to previous designs.

When we think of the ondol system, we usually associate it with a sedentary culture. However, from Goguryeo through Balhae to the Goryeo period, the ruling class favored a lifestyle centered around tables and beds rather than sitting on the floor. Even the ondol systems were not the full-length underfloor heating we see today, but rather partial heating. The widespread use of full-length floor heating emerged in the late Goryeo and early Joseon periods.

There are various theories about the origin of ondol heating systems, but the Goguryeo origin theory (including northern Okjeo) predominates, and Balhae's ondol heating systems were influenced by Goguryeo. Originally, ondol heating in Goguryeo was used by the poor. In the Biography of Goguryeo in the *Jiu Tangshu*, there is an account that says, "In their customs, there were many poor people. In winter, they would dig a long trench and light a fire under it to keep warm." Archaeologically, Goguryeo ondol heating systems are mainly found in common people's houses or military facilities in mountain fortress-

Entertain Guests (Wall Paintings of Tomb of the Dancers)

Master Couple (Wall Paintings of Tomb of the Twin Columns)

es. In addition, many Goguryeo murals depict the ruling class sitting on benches or chairs. In the Records of Goryeo (Ch. Gaoli tujing, 高麗圖經), it is said that while the kings and nobles of Goryeo used beds and low benches, commoners used earthen beds and partial hypocausts. This indicates that the ondol system was a heating method used by the poor.

In the case of Balhae, however, ondol systems are found in various types of residences, including those of the royal family, nobility, commoners, military facilities, and temples. It is clear that the people of Balhae had a real affinity for ondol heating regardless of social status. The ondol culture of Balhae influenced neighboring ethnic groups, so that Balhae-style ondol systems are found in the sites of Inner Mongolian and Jurchen peoples. Balhae was a pioneer in spreading the ondol system of heating throughout the Northeast Asia.

CHAPTER 7

LOST THE KINGDOM

22.
Collapsed Due to Eruption of Mt. Baekdu?

Kim Eunkuk

Various Causes of Balhae's Fall

At the turn of the 10th century, the last king of Balhae was King Dae Inseon (大諲譔), the 15th monarch. Balhae's downfall occurred about 20 years into his reign. The only record that sheds light on Balhae's downfall is found in the Biography of Yelu Yuzhi (耶律羽之傳) in the *Liaoshi* (遼史, History of Liao), which states, "[Khitan Taizi] moved, taking advantage of the schism created when [Balhae] was divided in their minds, and won without a fight (因彼離心 勝釁而動 不戰而克)."

Until now, research into Balhae's demise has been conducted with reference to this record. In essence, Balhae fell into disarray during the reign of King Dae Inseon, and amidst internal conflicts, it succumbed to a large-scale attack by the Khitans, leading to its downfall. The theory of self-destruction due to internal strife continues to have significant influence to this day.

However, there is no substantial evidence to support the theory of internal strife in Balhae. The theory itself is purely speculative. A key point often cited as evidence for this theory is the exile of the Balhae people to Goryeo, as mentioned in the *Goryeosa* (高麗史, *History of Goryeo*). There is a record stating that after the 8th year of King Taejo's reign in Goryeo (925), a large number of Balhae people from various walks of life sought refuge in Goryeo, especially prominent government and military officials. It is claimed that just before the collapse of Balhae, internal divisions among the ruling class caused a shift in public sentiment, leading some to flee to Goryeo. Seizing the opportunity, the Khitans launched a massive surprise attack that ultimately led to the fall of Balhae.

It should be noted, however, that the exile of the Balhae people to Goryeo was not limited to the time of Goryeo Taejo, but lasted for nearly 200 years until the reign of Goryeo Yejong in the 12th century. In addition, it should be kept in mind that the nature of historical records such as the *Liaoshi* favors a victor's perspective. Balhae was defeated in the war and again in the annals.

There are various interpretations of the fall of Balhae, but most of them are based on the records found in the *Liaoshi*, which serve to reinforce the theory of internal strife within Balhae. Consequently, the blame for the fall of Balhae is often placed on the Balhae people, especially the ruling class, with a special focus on the last king, Dae

Inseon. In this way, due to negative factors such as corruption, decline, and internal conflict in the late Balhae society, the fall of Balhae is equated with internal strife.

However, it is time to look at the fall of Balhae from a different perspective. Specifically, we should look at it from the perspective of the Balhae people, even though historical records are limited on this point. According to this perspective, the last king of Balhae engaged in active diplomacy during the period when the Khitans were expanding their influence. Balhae had interactions not only with the kingdoms of the Korean Peninsula, such as Silla and Goryeo, but also with neighboring regions such as China and Japan. It even had diplomatic exchanges with the Khitans themselves. It is recorded that Balhae formed alliances with several countries, including Silla, reflecting its efforts to prepare for the Khitan invasion.

Unfortunately, however, East Asia was in turmoil by the 10th century, and there were no states capable of responding to Balhae's requests. The existence and excavation of relics confirm that Balhae established a traditional defense system until its decline. Nevertheless, despite having a traditional military force, Balhae collapsed in the face of the large-scale Khitan attack. It can be assumed that this was because the Khitans had understood Balhae's traditional military strength.

Therefore, the Khitans targeted the Liaodong, to the west of Balhae's territory. Liaodong was a key strategic location in Northeast

Asia at that time, and its strategic importance is still significant today. The *Liaodong Xinbuzhi* (遼東行部志) also highlights the fact that the Khitans fought bloody battles against Balhae for decades before finally taking control of Liaodong. Having secured such a strategic foothold, the Khitans could easily conquer Balhae.

Based on the above discussion, we can summarize the causes of Balhae's downfall as follows: First, it cannot be attributed solely to internal conflicts or turmoil during Balhae's late period. The theory of internal strife is pure speculation. What is needed now is a perspective that focuses on Balhae itself when examining the fall of Balhae. This perspective can be found in the traditional defense system that Balhae maintained until its late period. In addition, the last king of Balhae, Dae Inseon, took both internal and external measures in response to the pressure from the Khitans. However, the surrounding states were unable to respond to Balhae's call for help.

Now is the time for a multifaceted understanding of the fall of Balhae. This is also necessary to shed new light on the movements for the revival of the Balhae people that unfolded throughout Balhae territory after the fall of the royal regime.

Volcanic Eruption of Mt. Baekdu as a Cause of the Fall of Balhae

Volcanic eruption have attracted widespread attention in recent years due to several notable eruptions. Against this background, claims have been made through various media that Mt. Baekdu (Ch. Changbaishan), will erupt in the near future. In particular, the eruption of Mt. Baekdu around the 10th century has attracted much attention because it is said to have led to the collapse of Balhae. These perspectives, mainly from the fields of geology and volcanology, focus on analyzing the volcanic ash of Mt. Baekdu to determine the age of the eruption.

Discussions linking the eruption of Mt. Baekdu to the fall of Balhae began in the early 1990s by the Japanese geologist Hiroshi Machida (町田洋). Even now, 30 years later, Machida's perspective seems to have been modified and refined. Initially, he tried to argue that the volcanic eruption of Mt. Baekdu, which occurred around 915, was directly related to the fall of Balhae in 926. However, as measurements of volcanic materials in Japan progressed, the timing of the volcanic eruption was adjusted to the 930s, after the fall of Balhae. This led to a different interpretation, suggesting that after the fall of Balhae by the Khitans, there were revival movements among the people of Balhae, but the eruption of Mt. Baekdu weakened their cohesion and eventually wiped out Balhae as a historical entity. Therefore, the eruption of Mt. Baekdu in the 10th century is not considered to be the direct cause of the fall of Balhae as proposed in Japan. Nevertheless, the Japanese geological community has focused on several eruptions that occurred in the period before and after that time, and is continuing research that considers the 9th-century eruption of Mt. Baekdu as a contributing factor that ultimately led to the collapse of Balhae.

Yoshinori Yasuda (安田喜憲), another volcano researcher in Japan, discussed the relationship between the environmental and historical events revealed by the technique of varve analysis, using the collapse of Balhae as an example. The varve analysis indicates that the eruption of Mt. Baekdu occurred later than the fall of Balhae. However, he theorized that there may have been sudden cooling of the climate three years before the fall of Balhae, suggesting that the Balhae people may have collapsed due to their inability to adapt to drastic climate changes.

Kazunobu Ikeya (地谷和信) also presented a similar perspective. He linked the sudden collapse of Balhae in 926 to the massive volcanic eruption of Mt. Baekdu, which resulted in volcanic material covering the territory of Balhae. In addition, he argued that radiocarbon dating placed the date of the eruption at approximately 920±20 years, leading him to describe the fall of Balhae as the "Pompeii of the East." These dating results are due to the fact that volcanic materials from the eruption of Mt. Baekdu were carried by prevailing winds across the East Sea to the Aomori region of northern Japan. This has been the core of the theory since the 1990s, which suggests that the eruptions of Mt. Baekdu caused the fall of Balhae.

Reinterpretation of the terms "離心 (divided minds) and "釁 (schism)"

It has already been discussed that the most detailed account of the fall of Balhae to date is the *Liaoshi*. Among its contents, the key passage is "因彼離心 勝釁而動 不戰而克" ("[the Khitan Taizi] moved, taking advantage of the schism created when [Balhae] was divided in their minds, and won without a fight"). While there have been transformative debates and discussions on the issues surrounding this passage, it still remains the basic textual evidence supporting the theory of internal strife. Furthermore, the newly proposed theory of Balhae's demise due to the eruption of Mt. Baekdu is advocated for on the basis of geological dating results. With the above considerations in mind, we aim to establish the following research direction.

First of all, there remains the challenge of bridging the gap between history and geology. This involves the interpretation of records related to Balhae and the historical documentation of various data. In addition, it should be assumed that the nature of the *Liaoshi* as a historical record to which all the data and interpretations presented converge. The *Liaoshi* is a historical record that focuses on the Khitans rather than the Balhae people. The fall of Balhae was also told from the Khitan perspective. I have previously noted that after being defeated in battle, Balhae suffered another defeat in the historical record. Thus, it may be worthwhile to reconsider the key passages "離心 (divided minds)" and "釁 (schism)" while keeping in mind that the

Khitans were the people who left the records. In other words, there is a possibility that the terms in question represent what the Khitans perceived to be the situation inside Balhae rather than what the Balhae leaders actually had in mind or what the real situation of Balhae was.

As for the term 離心, which has been interpreted as referring to the "divided minds of the Balhae leaders," it can be interpreted as the "rebellious minds of Balhae leaders" against the growing hostilities of the Khitans. This alternative interpretation may be justified by the escalation of hostilities between Balhae and the Khitans over Yoju (遼州) in 924, two years before the fall of Balhae. Although there are no records written by Balhae, records in the histories of Zhongyuan (中原) and surrounding states mention that Balhae and the Khitans competed for dominance over the Liadong region. The absence of any significant conflicts between the Khitans and Balhae after 924 indicates that the Khitans made a successful advance into part of the Liaodong region at the expense of Balhae, as recorded in the histories of the Five Dynasties. In fact, the Khitans, under the leadership of Yelu Abaoji, launched a full-scale attack against Balhae in 924 after conquering western Liaodong. In response, Balhae attacked Yoju and returned Balhae subjects there, thus demonstrating their "rebellious or hostile minds" against the aggressive Khitans.

Furthermore, the word 釁 (schism) may be interpreted in the context of the Khitans' attack strategy based on Balhae's defense vulnerability. Taking advantage of the limitations of Balhae's defensive strongholds, the Khitans attacked the capital city directly after winning the siege war at Buyeo Fortress. As a result, even the last line of defense led by No Sang crumbled, and when Sanggyeong of Balhae was subjected to a surprise night attack and encirclement, the last king of Balhae probably had no choice but to surrender for the sake of the majority of the Balhae people. I have previously mentioned that there is no record of battles between the Khitans and Balhae except for the siege of Buyeo Fortress. I believe that the Khitans' surprise attack on Sanggyeong was the final strategy of the Khitans.

Until now, the dominance of the Khitan-centric narrative in the interpretation of materials related to the fall of Balhae has caused Balhae to be perceived as a nation that collapsed on its own. In other words, while mistakenly recognizing the narrative subject as Balhae instead of the Khitans, there was a failure to consider the influence of the Khitan-centered perspective.

The limitations of these interpretations have finally intersected with the documentation of a series of volcanic material analysis data presented since the 1990s through research on the eruption of Mt. Baekdu. This has led to the emergence of a new area of interest in the study of the causes of Balhae's demise. Additionally, with the recent increase in global attention to climate change, the eruption of Mt. Baekdu has become an important issue for some scholars.

Now, it is imperative for the Korean historical community to also review and utilize the achievements of related disciplines such as geology to gather empirical data from each research field. These efforts will enable a more diverse and well-founded understanding of the causes of Balhae's downfall.

23.
Fierce Battle over Liaodong and the Fall of Balhae

Kwen Eunju

Fall of Balhae as a Historical Puzzle

Balhae suddenly collapsed in the first month of 926. It is considered a historical mystery that Balhae, once known as the *Flourishing Kingdom of the East* in the 9th century, fell within less than a month of the Khitan invasion. Because of this puzzle, there was a time when Balhae's internal strife was considered the reason for their abrupt fall, and the volcanic eruption of Mt. Baekdu also gained attention as a possible explanation. The internal strife theory is still discussed today, but it is not considered to be the main cause. Moreover, it has been proved that the volcanic eruption of Mt. Baekdu and the collapse of Balhae had nothing to do with each other. However, if one searches for the fall of Balhae on the internet, one will still find references to the eruption of Mt. Baekdu. Could it be because the fall of

Balhae is still considered a mystery?

To begin with the conclusion, Balhae did not suddenly collapse. For decades, Balhae fought bloody battles against the Khitans for the Liaodong region. During the reign of the last king, Dae Inseon, there were attempts to resolve the Khitan issue through active diplomacy, but Balhae could not avoid diplomatic isolation. Then, history records show that Balhae fell to the Khitan invasion. However, the details of this process are not thoroughly documented. We just know that Balhae collapsed within less than a month of facing a full-scale Khitan attack in the final war in which the capital was seized. Thus, the question remains as to whether there may be some hidden stories behind Balhae's collapse.

Khitan's Rise and Advance to Liaodong

Balhae and the Khitans did not have a strained relationship from the beginning. Balhae had a friendly relationship with the Khitans at the founding of the state. The deterioration of their relationship occurred when the Khitans began to flourish in the late 9th century, expanding their influence in the surrounding regions. In the process, power shifted within the Khitan leadership, and the Yelu Abaoji group emerged as a new force.

Born in 872, Yelu Abaoji made early forays into the northeastern region of today's China (northwest of Balhae). He launched attacks

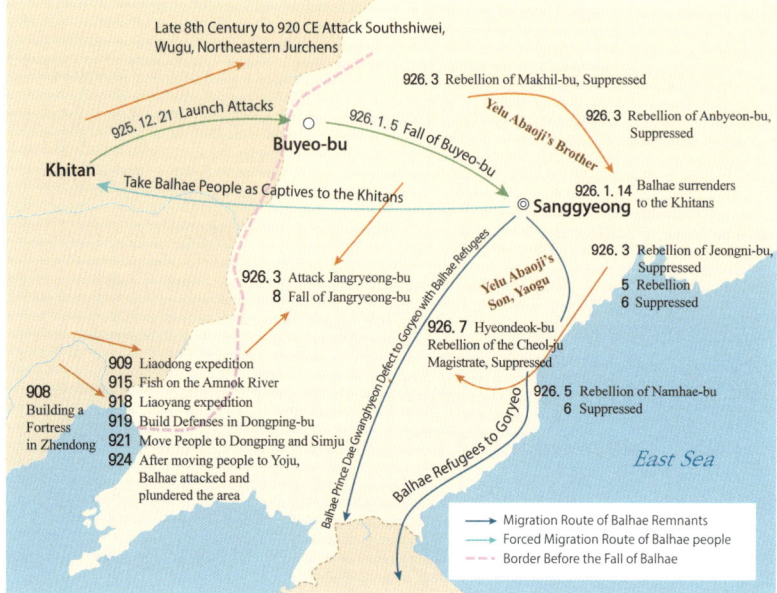

Khitan's Advance to Liaodong and Attacks on Balhae

on tribal groups such as Huangtou Shiwei (黃頭室韋), Yuewu (越兀), Wugu (烏古), and Northeastern Jurchen (東北女直), and brought them under his subjugation. By conquering these groups, he isolated the area of Buyeo-bu in the northwest of Balhae. Balhae stationed elite troops in Buyeo-bu to defend against the Khitans, making it a formidable region to conquer. Therefore, the Khitans wanted to control the surrounding areas to isolate Balhae and maintain a defensive foothold to prevent any attacks there.

Then, the Khitans made further inroads into the Liaodong region, the southwestern territory of Balhae. In 908, they built a long fortress in Zhendong (鎭東), presumably at the mouth of the Liao River, and used it as a base to cross the Liao River and control the area around today's Liaoyang. In 919, the Khitans appointed a defense commissioner to Dongping-jun (東平郡) in preparation for Balhae's attack from Jangryeong-bu and Amnok-bu. After that, the Khitans did not make any significant movements around the Liaodong region, except for relocating residents near Beijing to the Liaoyang region. Finally, in 924, Yelu Abaoji fulfilled one of his long-held ambitions(the conquest of the West and Balhae), and launched a large-scale attack on Balhae in the last month of 925. Balhae collapsed in the first month of the following year. This is the entirety of the historical record.

The Inscription of Chen Wan Reveals the Truth behind the Fall of Balhae

Although historical records are scarce, we now know that Balhae and the Khitans had been fighting over the Liaodong region and Balhae's northwestern territory since at least the early 10th century.

In addition, a tombstone inscription has been discovered that sheds light on the truth behind the fall of Balhae. The inscription belongs to Chen Wan (陳萬), who originally belonged to the Han (漢) ethnic group but surrendered to the Khitans and engaged in military activities. According to the tombstone inscription, Chen Wan followed Yelu Abaoji (Emperor Taizu of the Liao dynasty) to attack Balhae at the age of 45 (in 923), and joined Yelu Yaogu (later Emperor Taizong of the Liao dynasty) in the campaign against Balhae's Shinju and Hwanju at the age of 47 (in 925).

This information is not found in historical texts. The year 924, which falls between the two events of 923 and 925, is when Balhae attacked the Yoju (today's Liaoyang) after the Khitans moved the Chinese people there from the area of today's Beijing. This event is the only recorded counterattack by Balhae against the Khitan expansion into Liaodong.

The Khitans' consolidation of power and military strengthening in the Liaoyang area during their expansion into Liaodong had been evident since 909. It was puzzling that Balhae's response to this expansion did not occur until 924. However, Chen Wan's tombstone inscription provided the answer to this mystery. According to the inscription, Yelu Abaoji of the Khitans had already conducted a campaign against Balhae in 923, before Balhae's fall. However, the absence of this information in the records may be due to their failure in the face of Balhae's successful resistance.

When the attack on Balhae in 923 yielded little success, the Khitans probably moved the Chinese people who were taken in the Beijing area to Yoju in early 924 to strengthen their defenses. On the other hand, it is believed that Balhae retaliated for the 923 attack by launching an attack on Yoju in 924, killed its magistrate, and captured the residents. Failing to achieve success on the Balhae front and facing setbacks, the Khitans redirected their efforts to completing their Western Expedition first.

Then, in 925, Chen Wan followed Yelu Yaogu, the second son of Yelu Abaoji, back to the Balhae campaign. However, according to the records, Yelu Yaogu had participated in the Western Expedition in 924, but returned between the second and the fourth month of 925. He then followed his father, Yelu Abaoji, in his last major attack on Balhae in the twelfth month of the same year, where Balhae collapsed. Based on the timing, it is clear that Chen Wan's attack on Balhae's Shinju and other places in Amnok-bu with Yelu Yaogu took place between the fourth and the twelfth month in 925. Therefore, we can conclude that the war that led to the fall of Balhae had begun long before the twelfth month of 925.

The Yelu Agaoji's attack on Balhae was in the twelfth month of 925, but the war that ultimately led to the fall of Balhae had been going on for several months. Chen Wan's tombstone inscription revealed that Balhae did not fall within a month, contrary to what was previously believed.

24.
Revivalism of Balhae Refugees

Kim Jinkwang

In the early 10th century, the Tang dynasty, once hailed as the "Zhenguan Era of Prosperity (貞觀之治)" in the era of Emperor Taizong and the "Kaiyuan Era of Prosperity (開元之治)" in the era of Emperor Xuanzong, finally collapsed. The empire that brought about the fall of Goguryeo and saw Goguryeo remnants establish Balhae disappeared from history before Balhae's eyes. With the fall of the Tang dynasty, Zhongyuan (中原) fell into a disorder known as the Five Dynasties and Ten Kingdoms period, and the Khitans expanded their power and began a campaign of conquest. It was the same people, the Khitans, who had rebelled against the tyranny of the governor of Yingzhou in 696.

Yelu Abaoji, who united the Khitan tribes and expanded their territory, declared Balhae as their "enemy for generations" and launched invasions. It is known that Balhae had established Buyeo-bu on its border with the Khitans shortly after its founding, and stationed elite soldiers for defense. However, Balhae was unable to withstand the Khitan invasion, and within six days of the fall of Buyeo-bu, even its Sanggyeong was surrounded. Despite the fierce battle led by Balhae's General No Sang and his 30,000 soldiers between the fall of Buyeo-bu and the siege of Sanggyeong, the surrender of Dae Inseon marked the end of this chapter of history.

Balhae, once called the *Flourishing Kingdom of the East*, and praised with statements like "Three Balhae men are a match for a tiger," crumbled under the military operations of the Khitans within a few dozen days. The once-lofty military spirit vanished, and countless people, from the royal family to respected officials and even generals, left for Goryeo, Silla, the Turks, and Japan in search of a new life. However, the spirit of revival among the people who overcame their sorrows lasted for more than 200 years in various regions of the country. The signal for this revival was the establishment of Later Balhae.

Later Balhae, a Successor to Balhae

The revived state established on the basis of the resistance of the Balhae descendants is generally referred to as "Later Balhae (後渤海)." However, there is no clear consensus on who the founder of Later

Balhae was, when it was founded and fell, where its territory was located, and whether it had a fully developed state system. Later Balhae first appears in the records with the dispatch of an envoy to the Later Tang (後唐) in 929. However, it is unclear whether the envoy was sent as part of the revival movements that took place in many places after Dae Inseon's submission to the Khitans at Holhan Fortress, or as an initiative of Later Balhae in an effort to seek an alliance. As for its fall, there is a theory that it was absorbed into Jeonganguk (定安國), but another suggests that it survived until the year 1114. As for the geographical area where Later Balhae was active Sanggyeong Yongcheon-bu is speculated, but the Amnok River basin is also hypothesized. It is important to note, however, that the existence of the Later Balhae can be inferred from historical records, such as the way the Song dynasty referred to the Later Balhae envoys as "foreigners" or "your state," and the fact that they sent envoys to Zhongyuan (中原) several times and received the title of Governor of Namhae-bu.

Jeonganguk of the King Yeol Manhwa

The records of another revival state known as Jeonganguk can be found in the *Songshi* (宋史, History of the Song).

> Jeonganguk was originally composed of the Mahan people. When they were defeated by the Khitans, their leader gathered

the remaining group in the western border region and founded a state, which he called Jeonganguk. In 970, King Yeol Manhwa of Jeonganguk paid tribute and offered gifts through the Jurchen envoys. ... "Your subject O Hyeonmyeong, King of Jeonganguk, sends a message... I am originally a Balhae refugee from the ancient land of Goguryeo... In the past, however, the Khitans, believing in their strength and cruelty, invaded our land, destroyed our fortresses, and took our people captive. However, our ancestors did not surrender to the Khitans, but moved to another place and preserved the people."

This record indicates that Prince Taewon of Jeonganguk paid a tribute through Jurchen envoys in the second year of the Sunhwa, but there are no further record of this. According to this entry, the founder of Jeonganguk was Yeol Manhwa, the era name was Wonheung, and the name of the state was Jeonganguk. At some point, the king of Jeonganguk was replaced by O Hyeonmyeong. There is no consensus on whether the person known as the prince of Jeonganguk was the son of O Hyeonmyeong or someone else. However, Jeonganguk's location on the western border of the former Balhae area and the fact that its people were Balhae descendants suggest that it was one of the revival states that succeeded Balhae.

Heungryoguk of Dae Yeollim

Another important state in the revival of Balhae was Heungryoguk.

> The Khitan general of Dongjing (東京, Eastern Capital of Liao), Dae Yeollim, sent a high-ranking official, Go Gildeuk, to announce the founding of the state and to ask for help. Dae Yeollim, who was a seventh-generation descendant of Dae Joyeong, rose up in rebellion against the Khitans. He proclaimed the establishment of Heungryoguk and chose the reigning title of "Cheongyeong (天慶, heavenly joy)."
>
> - *Goryeosa* (高麗史), Seventh Month of the Twentieth Year of King Hyeongjong

Heungryoguk was founded by General Dae Yeollim in the ninth year of Khitan (Liao Dynasty) Emperor Xingzong (1029). Dae Yeollim was the Grand General of the Dongjing Liaoyang-bu. It is important to note that he identified himself as a descendant of Balhae and that this fact was known to Goryeo. This shows his determination to establish a state even after more than 100 years had passed since the fall of Balhae. The establishment of Heungryoguk is significant enough, even if it was prompted by the economic exploitation against the Balhae people.

Dae Yeollim's spirit of inheriting the tradition of Balhae can also be glimpsed in the name of the state, Heungryoguk (興遼國, State of Rising Liao). Since Liao dynasty already existed, the choice of Heung-ryo, meaning "State of Rising Liao," as the name of the state could be misunderstood as the revival of the Khitans. However, the fact that he claimed to be a seventh-generation descendant of Balhae's King Dae Joyeong and asked for help from Goryeo distinguishes the state name "Heungryo" from the Khitans' Liao. Perhaps the intention was to "recover the Liaodong region" and even beyond to "revive Balhae."

The Khitans employed strategies such as creating divisions among the Balhae descendants by appointing pro-Khitan men to important posts and blocking the Balhae people's resistance by dispersing the Balhae descendants. As a result, the newly established state of Heungryoguk, proclaimed in 1029, was completely subdued by the Khitans within a year. While confronting the Khitans, Dae Yeollim sent envoys to Goryeo five times, beginning with Dae Buseung and Go Gildeuk, then Dae Yeonjeong and Go Gildeuk, Dae Gyeonghan, and finally the governor of Yingzhou, Lee Gwangrok, to ask for military assistance. Sending envoys five times in one year indicates that the pressure of the Liao dynasty's military campaign was extremely strong. However, it was this spark that led to the rise of the Dae Balhaeguk.

Dae Balhaeguk of Go Yeongchang

Dae Balhaeguk (大渤海國, Great Balhae) arose at a time when the power of the Liao dynasty was waning. At that time, Aguda of Jurchen Wanyan united the Jurchen tribes and attacked the Khitans to establish a new dynasty known as the Jin (金). Goyok, a man of Balhae descent, raised anti-Khitan forces in Yaozhou, which is the upper reaches of the Shira Muren River in the Khitan heartland. He called himself the Great King, but the name of the state is unknown. Their activities lasted for five months before they were suppressed.

In 1116, a year after Goyok's failed rebellion, a revival movement under the leadership of Go Yeongchang developed in the Liaoyang region. The name of the state is recorded as Dae Balhae in the *Liaoshi*, while in the *Goryeosa* it is recorded as Daewon (大元, Great Yuan). Details about Go Yeongchang are not known, but he killed the governor of Donggyeong, defeated the military led by Dae Gongjeong and Go Cheongmyeong, and made the Donggyeong region his base. He then proclaimed himself emperor. The name of the state was Dae Balhae, and its era name was Yunggi (隆基, Rising Base) or Eungsun (應順, Reconciliation). Their revival movement expanded rapidly, taking over as many as 50 districts under the jurisdiction of Donggyeong. Dae Balhae even proposed an alliance with the Jin dynasty to attack the Liao dynasty. However, Jin demanded that Dae Balhae withdraw from the Liaodong region and give up his imperial title, and attacked Go Yeongchang. In the process, Eunsongno and Seonga betrayed Go Yeongchang, who was captured and subsequently killed by Nogeukchung.

The founding of Dae Balhae came long after the fall of Balhae. Economic exploitation by the Khitans had caused discontent among the Balhae people, and the power of the Liao dynasty had weakened enough to allow for the rise of a new dynasty, the Jin. The fact that Go Yeongchang, who inherited the royal family name of Goguryeo and an aristocratic family name of Balhae, aspired for the Great Balhae and strengthened the idea of inheriting the Balhae heritage is significant in the history of the Balhae revival movement.

After the fall of Balhae, the banner of revival continued to wave in the Balhae area. After hearing the news of Dae Inseon's surrender, the resistance led by Cheolli-bu and Jeongri-bu moved on to Dae Balhae via Jeonganguk and Heungryoguk. Many of the Balhae descendants who had been forcibly mobilized to Liaoyang became the driving force behind the revival movement, and their base, Donggyeong, became the holy land of the revival movement. They proclaimed themselves the descendants of Balhae and sought international solidarity to restore the glory of the *Flourishing Kingdom of the East*. Despite the setbacks caused by the Liao and Jin dynasties, they maintained the historical consciousness of the Balhae heritage, which has its own significance.

25.
Perceptions of the Goryeo Ruling Class toward Balhae

Kim Eunkuk

Distorted Perspective of China on Balhae Refugees

Research on Balhae history in Chinese academia treats Balhae as a part of Malgal, an ancient Chinese minority, rather than looking at its relationship with Goguryeo. In addition, they do not consider it important that many Balhae refugees entered Goryeo after the fall of Balhae, claiming that they were absorbed into the Liao dynasty of the Khitan and the Jin dynasty of the Jurchen and became part of the Chinese nation. The ultimate goal of the Chinese scholars seems to be to integrate Balhae into Chinese history.

Records such as the Goryeosa and the *Goryeosajeoryo* (高麗史節要, *Essentials of Goryeo History*) which document the history of Goryeo, mention that "after the fall of Balhae, when the Balhae prince Dae Gwanghyeon (大光顯) led tens of thousands of his remaining people to defect to Goryeo in the south, King Wang Geon (王建) of Goryeo expressed deep concern and treated them generously. He gave them family names and allowed them to continue their ritual ceremonies for the ancestors of the Balhae royal family. The official titles were also given to both civil and military officials of Balhae." These documents also record the history of Balhae refugees seeking asylum in Goryeo for nearly 200 years after the fall of Balhae, both before and after the year 926.

The massive migration of Balhae refugees to Goryeo would not have been possible without the connection between Balhae and Goryeo. However, the Chinese view of Balhae history attempts to deny even this connection. Chinese scholars argue that most of the Balhae descendants did not become part of Goryeo in the south, but rather assimilated into the Khitans, Jin, and Han Chinese, becoming an integral part of their respective ethnic groups.

Misunderstanding of the Balhae Refugees in Goryeo

In 2009, there was a Korean historical drama about the Queen Cheonchu (千秋太后), and the hype around it was quite intense even before it started. Before that, there was another drama called *Dae Joyoung*. What I realized then, and what is still true today, is that historical dramas tend to be judged more on the basis of the writer's creativity and ratings than on their accurate portrayal of historical facts.

While there is undoubtedly a positive aspect to a timely re-evaluation of certain aspects of history in our contemporary lives, we have, without realizing it, become more focused on the image of the actors portraying these roles. This has led to a recurring phenomenon in which plot development and the enjoyment of drama take precedence over historical accuracy. In the above-mentioned drama, the development of the royal lineages in early Goryeo, which had a confederate nature among the aristocracy, was portrayed as a rivalry between the Silla and Goryeo lineages, and the disharmony between Balhae refugees and Goryeo society was also emphasized. This inaccurate narrative has the potential to diminish Goryeo's place in Korean history.

As a researcher of Balhae history, I felt puzzled when I saw the scene in the drama where Balhae descendants incited a riot when Goryeo's King Gyeongjong (景宗) went to Pyongyang to attend a Buddhist festival, Palgwanhoe (八關會). I am well aware of the historical context in which Goryeo's founder, King Wang Geon, emphasized the dynasty's kinship with Balhae and considered the Khitans, which had defeated Balhae, as an enemy by expelling envoys sent by the Khitans and starving their present camels to death under Manbu Bridge (萬夫橋). I also recalled the historical account of Prince Dae Gwanghyeon, who led officials and commoners to seek asylum in Goryeo immediately after the fall of Balhae. The Goryeo royal family warmly welcomed them and allowed them to live in Hwanghae-do near the capital and continue their ritual ceremonies for the ancestors of the Balhae royal family.

The production team of this drama stated that in today's world, where various internal conflicts are deepening, the leadership of Queen Cheonchu, who embraced and united the Balhae refugees and led to a peaceful era in Goryeo, could serve as a model for us. However, I cannot help but wonder why they portrayed the Balhae refugees, whom Goryeo had already accepted, as rebels and even built a film set for the Balhae refugees that resembled a prison camp.

The people of Balhae were not merely defeated and passive, never to be considered citizens of a failed state. The fall of Balhae was merely an event in which the last king of Balhae surrendered to the king of the Khitans. Therefore, anti-Khitan resistance continued vigorously throughout the former territory of Balhae. This spirit was also reflected in the names of later states such as Later Balhae, Jeonganguk, Heungryeoguk, and Dae Balhae. The Balhae refugees continued to resist even after the fall of Balhae, and their resistance extended to later states such as Later Balhae and Jeonganguk.

The exile of the Balhae refugees, as recorded in the historical records of Goryeo, should be directly linked to the process of the Balhae refugees' resistance against the Khitans. The Balhae refugees who fled to Goryeo represented an unprecedented and prolonged period of migration in Korean history, lasting more than 200 years and involving tens of thousands, if not hundreds of thousands, according to historical records. It is impossible to understand the reasons for such a massive migration without considering the traditional kinship ties between Balhae and Goryeo. Incorrect perceptions of the Balhae refugees should not be ingrained in the entire history of Balhae. This is even more important than the distortions of Balhae history by outsiders.

Continued Journey of the Balhae Refugees

Although centuries had passed since the fall of Balhae, Balhae officials and citizens still called themselves Balhae people and sought refuge in Goryeo. Immediately after the fall of Balhae, King Wang Geon of Goryeo proposed a joint campaign to the Later Jin (後晉) against the Khitans, who had captured the king of Balhae. This was made possible by the kinship ties established through royal marriages between Balhae and Goryeo. The Balhae refugees, who came to Goryeo from all walks of life, played an important role in the unification of Goryeo and the Later Three Kingdoms. This was related to Goryeo's efforts to defend its northern borders after the fall of Balhae. Most of the records of Goryeo's territorial expansion during the Later Three Kingdoms period were concentrated in the northern region beyond the Han River. For Goryeo, accepting Balhae's refugees could have provided human and material resources to prepare against the Khitans. Therefore, it can be assumed that the Balhae refugees gradually settled and stably integrated into Goryeo society. The present-day surname Tae is related to the descendants of the Balhae people. The Balhae refugees throughout the Goryeo period can be described as a Korean "diaspora" that has continued from the fall of Balhae to the present day.

26.
Seven Generations of the Balhae Jang Clan

Kwen Eunju

A Balhae Remnant Jang Ho as the Highest Minister of the Jin

The *Jinshi* (金史, History of the Jin) mentions several Balhae descendants who played an active role in various fields such as politics, military, diplomacy, and culture. Among these individuals, Jang Ho (Ch. Zhang Hao) served five emperors in a row and even reached the highest position of the Jin, the prime minister.

According to the Biography of Jang Ho in the *Jinshi*, Jang Ho was from a family of Balhae descent in Liaoyang. His family was one of the powerful clans in the Liaoyang region among the Balhae survivors, who had been forcibly relocated there by the Khitans after their conquest of the Balhae kingdom in 926. However, according to the Biography, their original family name was Go (高氏), and they were descendants of King Dongmyeong (Jumong) of the Goguryeo founder. It is said that Jang Ho's ancestor, Jang Pae (張霸), changed the family name to Jang (張氏) when he entered government service. This indicates that the Jang Ho family had an identity as descendants of Balhae and traced their ancestry back to King Dongmyeong of Goguryeo.

Jang Ho played a crucial role in the establishment of the Jin dynasty by providing strategic advice to the founder of the Jin dynasty, Aguda, who trusted him and put him in charge of state documents. He continued to serve the emperors Taizong and Xizong in vital capacity of handling state documents and establishing state rituals. Jang Ho gained a reputation for his competent handling of tasks. For example, when a partisan Tian Gu (田穀) caused factional conflicts that paralyzed the government, Jang Ho managed to handle the work of six government ministries by himself, astonishing those around him. Even when he served as a regional governor to avoid factional conflict in the court, he was highly praised for his ability to maintain social order and stability.

Biography of Jang Ho in the *Jinshi*

During the reign of Emperor Hailing (海陵王), Jang Ho oversaw the construction of the Jin's capital Yangjing (燕京, or Zhongdu 中都).

He implemented a policy of ten-year tax exemptions for those who wished to relocate to the newly established city. This policy aimed at populating the city and laying the foundation for its growth. For his contributions, Jang Ho was appointed as the prime minister, a high-ranking government position. In the second year of Zhenglong era (1157), he was given the title of Nogukgong, an honorary title for his services. At this time, Jang Ho requested retirement due to old age and illness, but Emperor Hailing, recognizing the importance of his capable leadership, did not grant it.

However, as Emperor Hailing embarked on impellent construction projects and a campaign in the southern Song region, his relationship with Jang Ho began to distance itself. Despite Jang Ho's opposition, Emperor Hailing continued the campaign against the Southern Song and tragically lost his life during the expedition. When Emperor Shizong (世宗) ascended the throne, he also trusted Jang Ho and appointed him as the prime minister. When Jang Ho again expressed his intention to retire from politics, Emperor Shizong was concerned about his well-being and granted him a number of privileges such as exemption from kowtow, special seat reserved for him at palace, and even doing official business at home.

When Emperor Shizong had to make an important political decision, he always asked Jang Ho for his opinion. There is a remarkable example of how highly Emperor Shizong valued Jang Ho's advice. One day, Emperor Shizong asked Jang Ho, "Has there ever been a king in the past who abolished literature?" When Jang Ho replied, "Yes, there was," Emperor Shizong inquired, "Who was it?" Jang Ho replied, "It was the First Emperor of the Qin (秦始皇)." Upon hearing this, Emperor Shizong, who aspired to be a wise ruler, was so astonished that he never mentioned the abolition of the civil service examinations again. Unfortunately, this was Jang Ho's last achievement.

After Jang Ho's death in 1163, Emperor Shizong mourned his passing with great sorrow and temporarily suspended his royal duties. His funeral gifts to Jang Ho were bountiful, including 1,000 silver tael, a large amount of silk cloths, and a posthumous title. Moreover, even after the death of Shizong, Jang Ho was enshrined at the shrine of Shizong, and his portrait was dedicated to the Yanqing Palace (衍慶宮) in 1201.

Genealogical Chart on Epitaphs

In 1923, the tombstone of Jang Haengwon (張行愿), Jang Ho's father, was discovered at the tomb of the Dongjing (東京, Eastern Capital of Liao, today's Liaoyang). The discovery of this tomb inscription, along with the records in the *Jinshi*, revealed that the Jang Ho family had been a prominent lineage since the era of the Liao dynasty. Remarkably, the tombstone of Jang Ho's son, Jang Yeoyu (張汝猷), was also discovered in 1956 in today's Baiwanzhuang (白萬庄), Erligou (二里溝), Beijing.

While Jang Haengwon's epitaph has been known to the Korean scholarly community for some time, Jang Yeoyu's epitaph was only

Rubbing of Jang Haengwon's Epitaph

recently revealed. With the addition of Jang Yeoyu's tomb inscription, the genealogy and marriage connections of seven generations of the Jang Ho family have become even clearer. Such cases are extremely rare. The following table is the reconstructed genealogy of the Jang Ho family based on information from the *Jinshi*, and the epitaphs of Jang Haengwon and Jang Yeoyu.

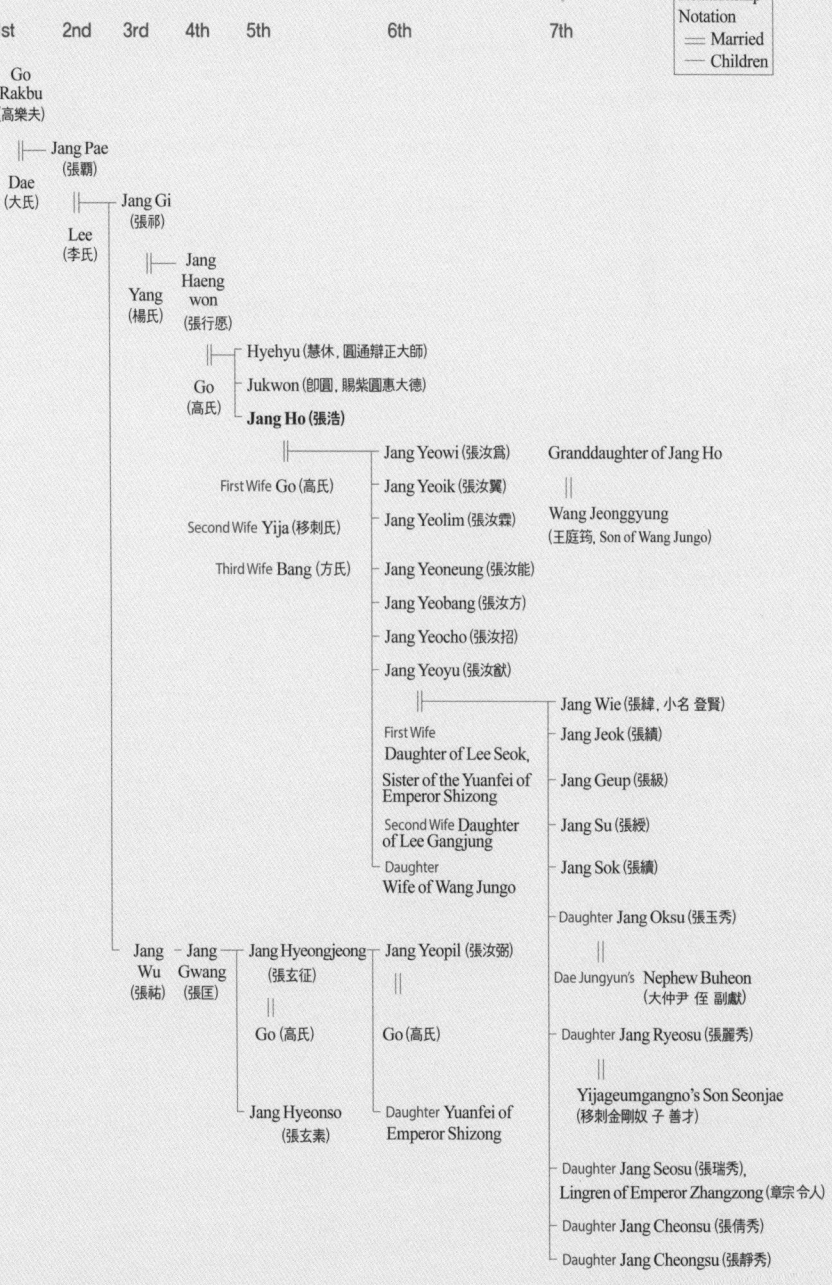

A notable passage in Jang Yeoyu's tombstone inscription reads, "Among prestigious and renowned families, the Jang family is the first in terms of contributions and honors." While tombstone inscriptions sometimes use exaggerated expressions to honor the deceased, in the case of the Jang Ho family, such a statement seems entirely appropriate. Jang Ho himself enjoyed the favor of the emperor for five generations, reaching the highest position of the prime minister. His sons also held positions as prime ministers and high-ranking officials, and they made marriages with the most powerful people.

Why Did the Jangs Marry Balhae Descendants?

The Balhae refugees enjoyed a high social status in the Jin dynasty and exerted considerable political and cultural influence. The period of Emperor Hailing, who married into a family of Balhae refugees, and Emperor Shizong who was praised as a wise king, are particularly noteworthy. The Jang family belonged to the core group of power during this period, and entered into marriages with influential people.

Jang Ho's son, Jang Yeoyu, married the daughter of Lee Seok, a fellow Balhae refugee. Lee Seok's sister was the Empress Zhenyi (貞懿 皇后), the birth mother of Emperor Shizong, and his daughter became *yuanfei* (元妃, Primary Concubine) of Shizong. Jang Yeoyu established a direct marriage relationship with the family of Shizong's maternal line. Jang Yeoyu's daughter, Jang Seosu, became a *lingren*

(令人, concubine) of Emperor Zhangzong (章宗). A sister from the same family became another Primary Concubine of Shizong. In this way, Jang Yeoyu's family established marriage relations with the Jin royal house or its consort clan.

A peculiarity of the Jang Ho family's marriages, however, is the frequent intermarriage with Balhae descendants. Their first known ancestor, Go Rakbu, married a Balhae woman with the surname Dae, while Jang Yeoyu's daughter, Jang Oksu married a Balhae man with the surname Dae. Jang Ho's daughter became the wife of Wang Zungo (王遵古), a Balhae refugee who was praised as the *Confucius of Liaodong*. Their son, Wang Jeongyun (王庭筠), was known for his literary distinction, and married to Jang Ho's granddaughter. In addition, the Yis, Yangs, and Gos that Jang Ho's clan married were most likely of Balhae descendants, as these surnames belonged to the aristocratic families of Balhae

Many centuries had passed since the fall of Balhae, so why did the Jang Ho family continue to intermarry with the descendants of Balhae? There could be two reasons. One was that they still identified themselves with a Balhae heritage. The Jang Ho family regarded themselves as the descendants of the Balhae and King Dongmyeong. Wang Jeonggyun even referred to himself as a Balhae descendant in his writings. It is well documented that the Balhae remnants of the Jin dynasty maintained a strong sense of Balhae identity. This may have influenced their intermarriage.

The other reason may have been that the Balhae descendants held considerable political power in the Jin dynasty. In the pre-modern class-based society, intermarriage among the elite to maintain their privileges was a common practice. Therefore, it can be assumed that the Jang Ho family's intermarriage with Balhae descendants had the dual purpose of preserving their Balhae identity and maintaining their social status as a privileged stratum in the Jin dynasty.

CHAPTER 8

LOSING THE HISTORY?

27.
How Can Balhae's Legacies Be Inherited?

Kim Eunkuk

Meaning of Balhae to Korea

Founded in 698, by former Goguryeo general Dae Joyeong, as,the successor state to Goguryeo, Balhae controlled a vast territory that included what are now the northeastern provinces of China, part of Yeonhaeju, and North Korea. Balhae lasted for 229 years, with fifteen kings in power, and enjoyed the reputation of the *Flourishing Kingdom of the East* until its royal line was suddenly ended by the surprise attack of Yelu Abaoji of the Khitans,

After the fall of Balhae, the activities of its remnants can be examined from a diasporic perspective in both time and space. Despite the surrender of the last king after the massive Khitan assault, the resistance efforts of the Balhae remnants, which lasted for over 200 years, are considered rare in world history.

Balhae played a central role in East Asia's transportation and trade by establishing routes such as the Silla Road, the Amnok Road, the Yingzhou Road to the Tang, the Khitan Road, and the Japan Road. Among these, the Silla Road stands out because it can shed light on the relationship between Balhae and Silla, focusing on the coastal regions of the East Sea.

In 700, shortly after founding his kingdom, King Go sent an envoy to Silla and Silla's King Hyoso bestowed on King Go *daeachan* (大阿湌)[8], a fifth-grade honorary position. This was not the highest rank, but not a low rank, reflecting Silla's perception of Balhae as a newly founded state. The *Samguk sagi* (三國史記, History of the Three Kingdoms), which recorded this event, referred to Balhae as *Bukguk* (北國, Northern Kingdom), marking the beginning of the era of Southern and Northern Kingdoms as envisioned by Yu Deukgong.

The archaeological remains of Balhae in the eastern coastal region have been mentioned in connection with the East Sea (Kr. Donghae 東海, Japan Sea) cultural area since prehistoric times. In particular, the Japan Road went from Sanggyeong through Donggyeong to modern-day Kraskino south of Vladivostok and then across the East Sea to Japan. Thus, the East Sea served as a kind of maritime highway linking the Asian continent and the Korean Peninsula with the Japanese archipelago. Balhae sent envoys to Japan 34 times, and Japan reciprocated

---

8   It is the fifth of the 17 gradws of Silla's official rank, and the royal nobility of Silla has it.

with 15 envoy missions to Balhae. These exchanges throughout the Balhae period illustrate Balhae's status as a maritime nation that simultaneously managed relations through both the land and the ocean. Examinin Balhae relics scattered northward from Cheongjin across the Duman River all the way to Yeonhaeju has brought new awareness to the importance of this region in the growth and expansion of Balhae.

Recently rediscovered gonu game boards also provide empirical evidence of Southern and Northern Kingdoms' exchange. The gonu boards, excavated in 2004 from the Balhae fortress of Yeomju (the area of modern-day Kraskino in Yeonhaeju) date back to the early 9th century. These boards are traditional Korean *cham*gonu boards, and their distribution can be traced from Jeju Island, through South Hwanghae-do in North Korea to the Yeomju in Yeonhaeju, north of the Duman River. Based on this, the concept of the Gonu Road has been established, reflecting the nature of the gonu game and gonu boards. This could serve as a new research topic in the field of the Southern and Northern Kingdoms.

Rise and Fall of Balhae as the Primary Mode of Diaspora in Korean History

• Dae Joyeong, the Founder of Balhae as the Resettlement Facilitator for the Goguryeo Diaspora

Dae Joyeong laid the foundation for the *Flourishing Kingdom of the East*, which lasted over 220 years. However, Dae Joyeong is not often portrayed in a diverse way in historical narratives. There are a few important considerations regarding terminology. First, we should apply the state name Balhae to Jinguk, since it was the starting point of Balhae. Second, Dae Joyeong should be referred to by his posthumous title King Go. It is important to recognize this change in terminology, which involves the use of the state name Balhae and the founder's posthumous title King Go.

• From Yingzhou to Mt. Dongmo to Found the State

The original name Jin associated with Balhae reflects another founding force and a major group within the country. Until now, the focus of the founding force has been on Yingzhou (near modern Chaoyang Municipality in Liaoning-sheng). During the same period as the Khitans' resistance against the Tang dynasty, Dae Joyeong led a migration of refugees to the east, defeated the Tang forces at Tianmen Pass, and established a kingdom at Mt. Dongmo. He then proclaimed the state of Jinguk. However, this process was made possible because the Jin forces around Mt. Dongmo and the Dae Joyeong forces from Yingzhou cooperated for 30 years after the fall of Goguryeo.

• Honglujing Stone Monument and Chinese Perception of Balhae

Even now, Chinese academics and private organizations are demanding the return of the Honglujing stone monument (鴻臚井碑) that Japan looted during the Russo-Japanese War. This stone monument had been built near today's Lushun at the southern tip of the Liaodong peninsula by a Tang envoy Cui Xin dispatched to Balhae in 713. After the Russo-Japanese War, it was moved to Japan's royal palace, including the outer part of the monument, and became known as Tangbeiting(唐碑亭). It is known as a Balhae monument because of the 29 Chinese characters engraved on it.

> The imperial commissioner to appease the Mohe (Kr. Malgal), Minister Honglu Cui Xin had the two wells [dug] as proof for good.
>
> The eighteenth day of the fifth month of the second year of the *Kaiyuan* era.
>
> - 勅持節宣勞靺鞨使 鴻臚卿崔忻井兩口永爲
>
> 記驗開元二年五月十八日.

The passage was inscribed on the stone monument, when the Tang envoy Cui Xin returned back to the Tang in 714. He had been dispatched for the purpose of winning over the Malgal. This passage has been cited until today by Chinese scholars as the basis on which they argue that Malgal was the earlier name of Balhae.

Chinese scholars explain that after Cui Xin's diplomatic mission in 713, Balhae abandoned the name Malgal and used only Balhae as its state name. They use this as evidence to claim that the Tang dynasty officially acknowledged Balhae's submission and incorporation under their rule. However, the prominent historical texts documenting the Tang dynasty, such as the *Jiu Tangshu* and the *Xin Tangshu*, clearly state that the founding title of Balhae was the *Jin* (振 or 震).

Chinese records attest to Balhae's status as the successor state to Goguryeo that the Goguryeo remnants founded by incorporating neighboring tribes. Thus, the term Malagal in the phrase "the imperial commissioner to appease the Mohe" can be interpreted as those Malgal groups who underwent incorporation by Balhae, and the whole phrase suggests a tone of relief on the part of the Tang because of the incorporation or subjugation of the potential threatening groups of people under Balhae's rule.

Last King, Dae Inseon, as the Primary Mode of Balhae Diaspora

• **Yelu Abaoji and the Small Fortress for the Balhae King**

According to the *Liaoshi*, Balhae's last king Dae Inseon, surrendered to Yelu Abaoji (Emperor Taizu of the Khitan Liao dynasty) on the first day of the first month in 926. In the seventh month of the same year, in the midst of continued resistance by the Balhae refugees, King Daeinseon was escorted to a fortress west of the imperial capital of the Liao, known as the Small Fortress for Balhae (渤海小城) or the Fortress for Dae Inseon (大諲譔城). Based on this record, the remains of the fortresses were recently identified. As an integral part of Sanggyeong of the Liao, the Small Fortress with rectangular ground was about 300 meters in length, while the interior structure had turned into a farm field and was severely damaged. Still, the remaining fortress wall in the north measures 180 meters long, and that in the west 130 meters relatively well preserved.

• **Perspectives on Balhae Descendants**

Another branch of the Balhae diaspora went to the south, to the kingdom of Goryeo to escape the rule of the Khitans. In response, King Taejo Wang Geon of Goryeo emphasized his kinship with Balhae and regarded the Khitans, who had destroyed Balhae, as enemies. In particular, he sent the Khitan envoys into exile, and the camels they had brought were left to starve under the Manbu Bridge in Gaeseong. In addition, soon after the fall of Balhae, when Prince Dae Gwanghyeon of Balhae led the officials and people to seek asylum in Goryeo, they were given places in Hwanghae-do to perform ceremonial rituals for Balhae royal ancestors.

The fall of Balhae was merely an event in which the last king of Balhae surrendered to the Khitan king. After that, a fervent anti-Khitan resistance continued to unfold in former territory of Balhae. Its traces remain in the names of later states, such as Later Balhae, Jeonganguk, Heungryoguk, and Dae Balhae. The migration of Balhae refugees to Goryeo, as recorded in the *Goryeosa*, should be understood in the context of the Balhae diaspora and their resistance to the Khitans.

The historical domain of Balhae currently spans China, Russia, and North Korea, and research on Balhae history is expanding its scope to include Japan and Mongolia. Exploration and research of Balhae archaeological sites under the protection of each country can expand our understanding of the extent of Balhae diaspora activities through relics and artifacts. It can also contribute to a more objective framework for perceiving Balhae history, moving away from a nation-centred perspective and adopting a diasporic approach. In this way, it will be possible to establish the significance of Balhae's history in the context of East Asian regional history.

Balhae as the *Flourishing Kingdom of the East* lasted for over

220 years and, saw its royal line disrupted by the Khitan invasion during the reign of its last king. There were various causes of Balhae's downfall, but it is widely believed that changing circumstances in East Asia, including the rise of the nomadic Khitan people, were significant factors. Just as important as the fall of Balhae is the resurgence of Balhae refugees, research on whom can play a significant role in Balhae studies. This resurgence movement can be seen in parallel with the resurgence of Goguryeo refugees after the fall of Goguryeo, serving as a precursor to the diaspora of the Korean people.

After the fall of Balhae, Korea's territorial boundary has been confined to south of the Amnok and Duman Rivers for over 1,000 years. In South Korea, Balhae is confidently recognized as a part of Korean history. In reality, however, Balhae's relics and artifacts are under the management of North Korea, Russia, and China. The participation of South Korean scholars in the excavation and study of Balhae archaeological sites in these regions is absolutely necessary. At present, South Korean scholars are jointly participating in the excavation of Balhae relics in Yeonhaeju of Russia. In this regard, it is hoped that discussions and agreements can be reached with North Korea and China to expedite South Korean participation in the excavation of Balhae relics in these regions as well.

Genealogical Chart of the Balhae Kings

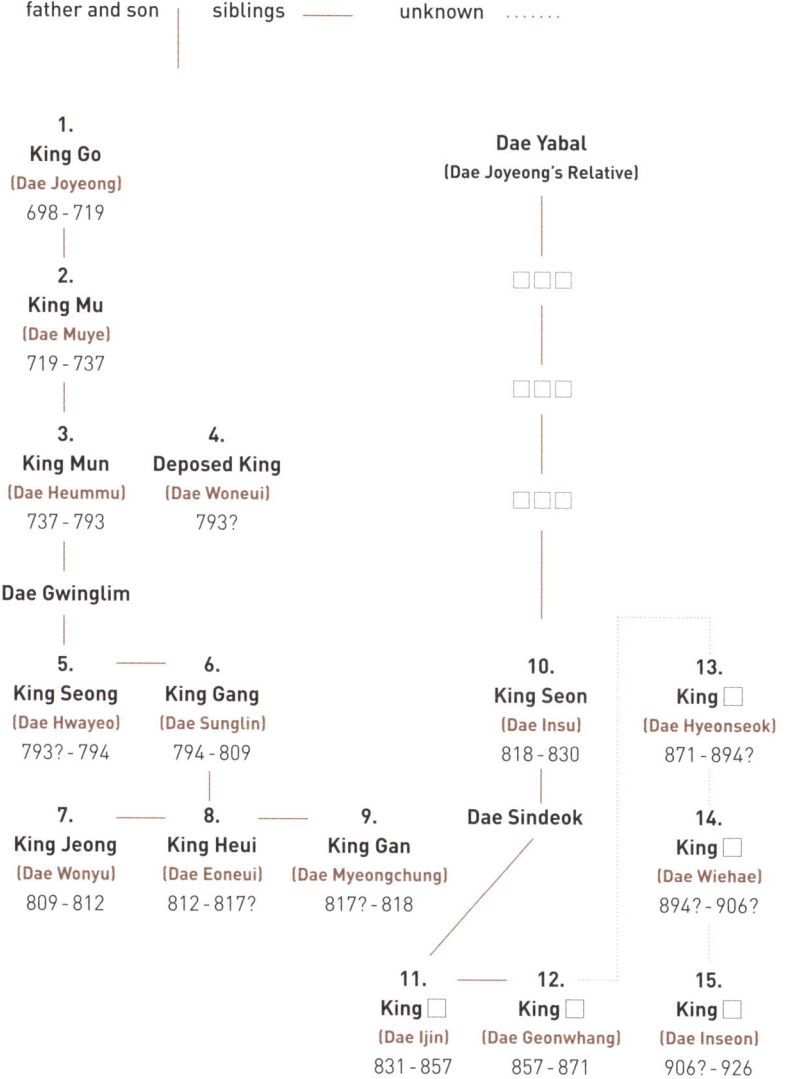

Timeline of Pre-modern Korean History

century	period(Age)	state name	note
BCE 20nd~ BCE 3nd	Bronze	Former Gojoseon	Dangun Joseon (BCE 2333 ?~?)
BCE 3nd~	Iron	Later Gojoseon	Wiman Joseon (BCE 194~BCE 108)
BCE 2nd~ AD 3nd	Proto-Three Kingdoms	Buyeo, Okjeo, Dongye, Proto-Goguryeo, Three Han (韓: Mahan, Jinhan, Byeonhan)	Han(漢) Commanderies (BCE 108)
4nd~7nd	Three Kingdoms	Silla(BCE 57~) Goguryeo(BCE 37~668) Baekje(BCE 18~660) Gaya(42~562)	Silla's unification (676)
8nd~ the first quarter of 10nd	Northern and Southern Kingdoms	Unified Silla Balhae(698~926)	
10nd~14nd	Later Three Kingdoms	Silla(~936) Later Goguryeo(901~918) Later Baekje(900~936)	Goryeo's unification (936)
	Goryeo	Goryeo(918~1392)	
14nd~19nd	Joseon	Joseon(1392~1897)	the Korean Empire (1897~1910)

Bibliography

Korean Language Materials

Collections of Historical Materials

Kim Yukbul, ed. Balhaesa Yeonguhoe (Research Society for the history of Balhae), trans. 2008. Sinpyeon Balhaegukji jangpyeon (New edition of compilation of the researches and materials on the Balhae state). Seoul: Sinseowon.

Northeast Asian History Foundation, ed. 2007. Balhaesa jaryojip (Collection of materials for the history of Balhae), vol. 1 and vol. 2. Seoul: Northeast Asian History Foundation.

Monographs

Han Gyucheol. 1994. Balhae eui daeoe gwangyesa (History of Balhae's foreign relations). Seoul: Sinseowon.

Han Gyucheol, et al. 2007. Balhae 5 gyeong gwa yeongyeok byeoncheon (Five capitals of Balhae, and changes in its territories). Seoul: Northeast Asian History Foundation.

Jeong Byeongjun, et al. 2011. Jungguk eui Balhae daeoe gwangyesa yeongu (Study on the history of China's relations with Balhae). Seoul: Northeast Asian History Foundation.

Ku Nanhee. 2017. Balhae wa Ilbon eui gyoryu (Exchange between Balhae and Japan). Seongnam: Academy of Korean Studies Press.

Kim Eunkuk, et al. 2017. Balhae Yeomjuseong iyagi—Dong Asia eui munhwa heobeu (Story of Balhae's Yeomju Fortress: A cultural hub of East Asia). Seoul: Cheonga chulpansa.

Kim Jinkwang. 2012. Balhae Mun wang dae eui jibae cheje yeongu (Study on the ruling system of Balhae King Mun). Seoul: Bakmunsa.

Kim Jinkwang. 2012. Bukguk Balhae tamheom (Exploration of a northern state Balhae). Seoul: Bakmunsa.

Kim Jongbok. 2009. Balhae jeongchi oegyo sa (Political and diplomatic history of Balhae). Seoul: Ilchisa.

Lee Byeonggeon. 2003. Balhae geonchuk eui ihae (Understanding Balhae's architecture). Seoul: Baeksan jaryowon.

Lee Hyohyeong. 2007. Balhae yuminsa yeongu (Study on the history of Balhae remnants). Seoul: Hyean.

Lee Hyohyeong, et al. 2009. Dong Asia eui Balhaesa jaengjeom bigyo yeongu (Comparative study on the controversial points over the history of Balhae among East Asian countries). Seoul: Northeast Asian History Foundation.

Lim Sangseon. 1999. Balhae eui jibae seryeok yeongu (Study on the ruling powers of Balhae). Seoul: Sinseowon.

Na Yeongnam. 2017. Yo·Geum sidae iminjok jibae wa Balhae (Control over foreign peoples including Balhae people in the Liao and Jin eras). Seoul: Sinseowon.

Northeast Asian History Foundation, ed. 2007. Balhae eui yeoksa wa munhwa (Balhae's history and culture). Seoul: Northeast Asian History Foundation.

Northeast Asian History Foundation, ed. 2007. Saeropge bon Balhaesa (A new history of Balhae). Seoul: Northeast Asian History Foundation.

Northeast Asian History Foundation, ed. 2010. Godae hwan Donghae gyoryusa—2 bu (History of ancient communications across the East Sea, Part II). Seoul: Northeast Asian History Foundation.

Shavkunov, Ernest V, ed. Song Giho and Jeong Seokbae, trans. 1996. Reosia Yeonhaeju wa Balhae yeoksa (Yeonhaeju, and the history of Balhae). Seoul: Mineumsa.

Song Giho. 1995. Balhae jeongchisa yeongu (Study on the political history of Balhae). Seoul: Ilchogak.

Song Giho. 2011. Balhae sahoe munhwa sa yeongu (Study on the social and cultural history of Balhae). Seoul: Seoul National University Press.

Wang Chengli. Song Giho, trans. 1987. Balhae eui yeoksa (History of Balhae). Chuncheon: Asia munhwa yeonguso, Hallym University.

Yun Jaeun. 2006. Hanguk godae muyeoksa yeongu (Study on the history of trade in ancient Korea). Seoul: Gyeongin munhwasa.

Yun Jaeun. 2015. Gyoryu eui bada Donghae (The East Sea, a sea of interstate relations). Seoul: Gyeongin munhwasa.

Articles

Baek Jongo. 2015. "Balhae giwa yeongu eui chui wa myeot gaji dansang" (Trends of study on Balhae's roof tiles, and some ideas). Koguryo Balhae yeongu 52. Seoul: Koguryo Balhae hakhoe.

Bang Gyeongil. 2006. "Geumdae myojimyeong e sillin Balhae yumin" (Balhae remnants as seen in the epitaphs from the Jin era). Baeksan hakbo 76. Seoul: Baeksan hakhoe.

Han Gyucheol. 2006. "Balhae eui yeongyeok eseo bon Koguryo gyeseungseong" (Balhae's succession to Koguryo in terms of its territories). Koguryo Balhae yeongu 22. Seoul: Koguryo Balhae hakhoe.

Han Gyucheol. 2015. "Samguk gwa Balhaesa eseoeui Malgal" (Malgal in the histories of Three Kingdoms and Balhae). Hanguksa hakbo 58. Seoul: Goryeosa hakhoe.

Jeon Hyeonsil. 2004. "Daeoe gyoryu eseo natanan Balhae eui euiryo gochal—dae Dang dae Il gwangye reul jungsim euro" (Study on the textiles of Balhae as seen in its interstate relations: Focusing on its relations with the Tang and Japan). Seonsa wa godae 21. Seoul: Hanguk godae hakhoe.

Jeong Seokbae. 2011. "Yeonhaeju Balhae sigi eui yujeok bunpo wa Balhae eui dongbuk jiyeok yeongyeok munje" (Balhae remains in Yeonhaeju, and its territories in the northeastern region). Koguryo Balhae yeongu 40. Seoul: Koguryo Balhae hakhoe.

Kang Seongbong. 2015. "Balhae geumgun gwa doseong bangeo chegye" (Balhae's royal guards and the capital defense system). Yeoksa wa hyeonsil 97. Seoul: Hanguk yeoksa yeonguhoe.

Kim Eunkuk. 2007. "Jungguk eui Dongbuk gongjeong sang e boineun Balhae sa seosul" (Chinese description of the history of Balhae according to its Northeast Project). Asia munhwa yeongu 12. Seongnam: Kyungwon University.

Kim Eunkuk. 2008. "Deungju reul jungsim euro han Balhae wa Dong Asia eui gyoryu" (Balhae's exchange with East Asia Centered on Dengzhou). Dong Asia godaehak 17. Seoul: Dong Asia godae hakhoe.

Kim Eunkuk. 2008. "Balhae wa Ilbon eui gyoryu wa Kraskino seong" (Exchange between Balhae and Japan, and the Balhae Fortress at Kraskino). In Dong Asia sok eui Balhae was Ilbon (Balhae and Japan in the Context of East Asia). Seoul: Gyeongin munhwasa.

Kim Eunkuk. 2010. "Kraskino seong gwa Fukura hang" (Balhae fortress at Kraskino and the Fukura port). In Godae hwan Donghae gyoryusa—2 bu (History of ancient communications across the East Sea, Part II). Seoul: Northeast Asian History Foundation.

Kim Eunkuk. 2011. "Nambukguk sidae ron gwa Balhae Diaspora" (Thesis of the Southern and Northern Kingdoms Period, and Balhae Diaspora). Koguryo Balhae yeongu 35. Seoul: Koguryo Balhae hakhoe.

Kim Eunkuk. 2013. "Balhae eui hwan Donghae gyoryu wa Yeonhaeju" (Balhae's communications across the East Sea, and the Yeonhaeju). Baeksan hakbo 97. Seoul: Baeksan hakhoe.

Kim Eunkuk. 2014. "Han Mong Balhae yujeok gwa 'gonu—gil'" (Balhae remains in Korea and Mongolia, and the 'gonu'—Road). Yeoksa minsokhak 46. Seoul: Hanguk yeoksa minsok hakhoe.

Kim Eunkuk. 2015. "Balhae Yeomju seong balgul eui jeongae wa banghyang" (Excavation of Balhae's Yeomju Fortress and Its Direction). Chung-Ang saron 42. Seoul: Chung-Ang sahak yeonguso at Chung-Ang University.

Kim Eunkuk. 2016. "Choegeun 10 nyeongan Balhae sa yeongu eui hoego wa jeonmang" (Recollection of study on Balhae history over the past ten years, and its prospect). Dongbuk A yeoksa nonchong 53. Seoul: Northeast Asian History Foundation.

Kim Eunkuk. 2017. "Balhae Yeomju seong eui choegeun balgul seonggwa wa bunseok" (Analysis of the recent excavation of the Balhae Yeomju Fortress). Koguryo Balhae yeongu 58. Seoul: Koguryo Balhae hakhoe.

Kim Eunkuk. 2018. "Donghae reul neomna deulmyeo bokwon han Balhae wa Ilbon gwangyesa yeongu" (Reconstruction of Balhae-Japan relations through field studies across the East Sea). Koguryo Balhae yeongu 61. Seoul: Koguryo Balhae hakhoe.

Kim Jinkwang. 2004. "Balhae geonguk chogi eui gangyeok—Yeongjudo reul jungsim euro" (Territory of Balhae in its early years: Focusing on the Yingzhou route). Seonsa wa godae 21. Seoul: Hanguk godae hakhoe.

Kim Jinkwang. 2008. "Balhae geonguk jipdan eui seonggyeok" (Characteristics of the founding group of Balhae). Hanguksa yeongu 143. Seoul: Hanguksa yeonguhoe.

Kim Jinkwang. 2008. "Seoksilmyo joyeong eul tonghae bon Balhae eui bukbang gyeongyeong" (Balhae's northern rule as seen through the construction of stone chamber tombs). Koguryo Balhae yeongu 30. Seoul: Koguryo Balhae hakhoe.

Kim Jinkwang. 2010. "Seogoseong eui gungjeon baechi reul tonghae bon Balhae toseongje eui byeonhwa" (Changes in Balhae's capitals as seen in the arrangement of royal palace in the Xiguchen 西古城). Koguryo Balhae yeongu 38. Seoul: Koguryo Balhae hakhoe.

Kim Jinkwang. 2012. "Hongjuneojang gobungun eui sahoe jeok jiwi mit seonggyeok: gobungun eui yuhyeong gwa bunpo sanghwang eul jungsim euro" (Social position and characteristics of the Hongzun yuchang 虹鱒漁場 tomb complex: Focusing on the types and distributions of tombs). Koguryo Balhae yeongu 42. Seoul: Koguryo Balhae hakhoe.

Kim Jinkwang. 2012. "Balhae toseong eui gujo wa hyeongseong gwajeong e daehan gochal" (Examination of Balhae capitals' structure and their formation process). Munhwajae 45-2.

Seoul: Guknip munhwajae yeonguso.

Kim Jinkwang. 2015. "Balhae wa Malgal gwangye eui yeongu hyeonhwang gwa gwaje" (Current status and research subjects of Balhae-Malgal relations). Minjok munhwa nonchong 60. Gyeongsan: Minjok munhwa yeonguso, Yeongnam University.

Kim Jinkwang. 2016. "Yi Seunghyu Jewang ungi eui Gogurye·Balhae insik" (Perceptions of Yi Seunghyu's Jewang ungi 帝王韻紀 (Songs of emperors and kings) toward Koguryo and Balhae). Minjok munhwa nonchong 64. Gyeongsan: Minjok munhwa yeonguso, Yeongnam University.

Kim Jinkwang. 2018. "Jungguk hakgye eui Balhae gobun yeongu hyeonhwang gwa jaengjeom" (Current status and controversial points of Chinese scholars' study on Balhae's tombs). Koguryo Balhae yeongu 60. Seoul: Koguryo Balhae hakhoe.

Kim Jinkwang. 2018. "Balhae Yongdusan gobungun Yonghae guyeok M13·M14 gobun eui wisang geu juingong e daehan siron jeok gochal" (Preliminary examination on the status and owners of the tombs (M13 and M14) in the Longhai 龍海 district of the Mt. Longtou 龍頭山 tomb complex). Seonsa wa godae 56. Seoul: Hanguk godae hakhoe.

Kim Jinkwang. 2018 "Manju wonryu go eui jeongeo jaryo wa Balhae gangyeok e daehan seolsul taedo" (Source materials of the Manzhou yuanliu kao 滿洲源流考 (Study on Manchu origins) and its perspective in describing Balhae's territory). Seonsa wa godae 58. Seoul: Hanguk godae hakhoe.

Kim Musik. 2008. "Balhae munja eui seongnip gwa munjaron jeok teukjing" (Establishment of Balhae characters and their characteristics). Eoneo gwahak yeongu 47. Seoul: Eoneo gwahak hakhoe.

Ku Nanhee. 2013. "Balhae wa Ilbon eui gyoryu hangno byeonhwa e gwanhan yeongu" (Study on the changes in the sea routes between Balhae and Japan). Yeoksa gyoyuk 126. Seoul: Yoksa gyoyuk yeonguhoe.

Ku Nanhee. 2017. "Balhae Donggyeong jiyeok eui yeoksa jeok yeonwon gwa jiyeokseong" (Historical origin and local nature of Balhae's Eastern Capital). Koguryo Balhae yeongu 58. Seoul: Koguryo Balhae hakhoe.

Kwen Eunju. 2009. "Malgal 7 bu eui silche wa Balhae waeui gwangye" (Seven provinces of Malgal and their relations with Balhae). Koguryo Balhae yeongu 35. Seoul: Koguryo Balhae hakhoe.

Kwen Eunju. 2010. "7 segi huban bukbang minjok eui ban Dang hwaldong gwa Balhae geongu" (Anti-Tang movements of the northern peoples in the latter half of the seventh century, and the founding of Balhae). Baeksan hakbo 86. Seoul: Baeksan hakhoe.

Kwen Eunju. 2011. "8 segi mal Balhae eui cheondo wa bukbang minjok gwangye" (Move of the Balhae's capital in the late eighth century, and its relations with the northern peoples). Koguryo Balhae yeongu 41. Seoul: Koguryo Balhae hakhoe.

Kwen Eunju. 2012. "Balhae Mu wang dae yeongyeok hwakjang gwa bukbang jeongse byeondong" (Balhae's expansion of territory in the era of King Mu, and the changes of political situations in the northern region). Koguryo Balhae yeongu 43. Seoul: Koguryo Balhae hakhoe.

Kwen Eunju. 2013. "Balhae eui Deungju gonggyeok eul tonghae bon gukje dongmaeng gwa oegyo" (International alliance and diplomacy seen through Balhae attack on Dengzhou). Yeoksa wa sege 44.

Kwen Eunju. 2014. "Koguryo yumin Go Heumdeok, Go Heummang buja myojimyeong geomto" (Examination of the epitaphs of Koguryo remnants Go Heumdeok and his son Go Heummang). Daegu sahak 116. Daegu: Daegu sahakhoe.

Kwen Eunju. 2016. "Balhae sa yeongu, geumseokmun mannada" (Study of the history of Balhae through stone and metal inscriptions). Bokhyeon sarim 34. Daegu: Gyeongbuk sahakhoe.

Kwen Eunju. 2016. "Balhae was Georan gyeonggye eui siron jeok geomto" (Preliminary study on the borders between Balhae and the Khitans). Koguryo Balhae yeongu 54. Seoul: Koguryo Balhae hakhoe.

Kwen Eunju. 2016. "Dang dae Yeongju chulsin Koguryo gye Go Yeongsuk eui myojimyeong geomto" (Review of the epitaph of Go Yeongsuk of Koguryo decent at Yingzhou of the Tang). Hanguk godaesa yeongu 84. Seoul: Hanguk godaesa hakhoe.

Kwen Eunju. 2018. "Bal·Il 'gukseo' bunjaeng gwa 'Jungdaeseong cheop'" (Dispute between Balhae and Japan over the state letters, and the communication letters of the Central Secretariat). Daegu sahak 133. Daegu: Daegu sahakhoe.

Lee Byeonggeon. 2011. "Geonchuk jeok gwanjeom eseo bon Balhae yujeok e daehan Hanguk eui yeongu dongyang" (Research trend of the studyon Balhae remains from the viewpoint of architecture). Koguryo Balhae yeongu 41. Seoul: Koguryo Balhae hakhoe.

Lee Hyohyeong. 2015. "Balhae yuminsa gwallyeon gogohak jaryo eui geomto" (Examination of archaeological materials related to the history of Balhae remnents). Koguryo Balhae yeongu 52. Seoul: Koguryo Balhae hakhoe.

Lim Sangseon. 2006. "Balhae eui Donggyeong e daehayeo" (On Balhae's Eastern Capital).

Koguryo Balhae yeongu 25. Seoul: Koguryo Balhae hakhoe.

Lim Sangseon. 2010. "Balhae eui wangdo Hyeonju wa Junggyeong chiso Seogoseong eui gwangye" (Balhae capital Hyeonju, and its relations with Xigucheng of Junggyeong). Koguryo Balhae yeongu 37. Seoul: Koguryo Balhae hakhoe.

Song Giho. 2006. "Tongil Silla sidae eseo Nambukguk sidae ro" (From the Unified Silla period to the Southern and Northern Kingdoms period). Yeoksa bipyeong 74. Seoul: Yeoksa bipyeongsa.

Song Gigho. 2010. "Yonghae guyeok gobun balgul eseo deureonan Balhaeguk eui seonggyeok" (Characteristics of the Balhae state as seen in the tombs excavated in the Longhai 龍海 district). Koguryo Balhae yeongu 38. Seoul: Koguryo Balhae hakhoe.

Song Giho. 2012. "Haeoe yujeok gwa Yeonhaeju josa" (Overseas [Balhae] remains, and investigation of [Balhae remains] in Yeonhaeju). 2012 Asia Archaelogy gukje haksul symposieom (International academic symposium on Asia archaeology, 2012). Seoul: Guknip munhwajae yeonguso.

Yang Sieun. 2015. "Yeonhaeju jiyeok Balhae eui jibang jibae bangsik yeongu" (Study on Balhae's local control in the Yeonhaeju region). Hoseo gogohak 33. Asa: Hoseo gogo hakhoe.

Yun Jaeun. 2011. "Balhae eui 5 gyeong gwa gyotongno eui gineung" (Balhae's five capitals, and function of the transportation routes). Hanguk godaesa yeongu 63. Seoul: Hanguk godaesa hakhoe.

Yun Jaeun. 2013. "Jungguk eui Balhaesa woegok nolli wa daeeung bangan"(Chinese distortion of the history of Balhae, and reaction measures against it). Hanguksa hakbo 51. Seoul: Goryeosa hakhoe.

Yun Seontae. 2007. "Balhae munja jaryo eui hyeonhwang gwa gwaje" (Current status and research subjects of Balhae's literary materials). Daedong hanmunhak 26. Seoul: Daedong hanmun hakhoe.

Index

5 Gyeong(京, capital), 15 Bu(府, Provinces), 62 Ju(州, county) 57, 125

Aguda 210, 219
Ammohwa (暗摸靴) 163
Amnok Road 121, 229
An Lushan 74, 75, 85
Anbyeon-bu 56, 82, 95, 200
Angeogol 54
An-Shi rebellion 75, 76, 78, 85, 86
Anwon-bu 57, 95, 126
Aomori 193

Bae Gu (裵璆) 168, 175
Bae Jeong (裵頲) 105, 175, 176
Baekdol 54
Baeksan 54
Baiwanzhuang (白萬庄), Erligou (二里溝) 221
Balhae 1300 Raft 31
Balhae Jungdaeseong chi Nihon Daijōkan cheop (Letters of the Central Office of Balhae, Addressed to the Bureau of Great Council of Japan) 140
Balhae Malgal 38~41
Balhaego (渤海考, Study of Balhae) 23, 26, 156
Balhaegwan (渤海館, Balhae Office) 119
Baliancheng 84, 87, 125
Battle of Ansi 35
battle of Mt. Madou 70, 71
Bingongke (賓貢科) 23
Biography of Jang Ho 218, 219
Biography of Yelu Yuzhi (耶律羽之傳) 188
Bird-feather headgear 25
Biwi (羆衛, Big Bear Guard) 148
Black sable (黑貂) 121, 168
Black Sable (黑貂) Road 121
Bokdu (幞頭) 162
Boryeok (寶曆, Valuable Era) 57, 61, 62, 145
Buddhist dharma king 145
Bugeo-ri 117, 118

Bugyeong (桴京, granaries) 178
Bukcheong Earthen Fortress 117
Bukdae tomb complex 84
Bukguk (北國, Northern Kingdom) 229
Bulyeol 54, 56, 95, 96~98, 101, 126
Bulyeol Malgal 96~98
Buyeo Fortress 196
Buyeo-bu 51, 56, 82, 95, 124, 125, 200, 205

Carp of the Mita Lake 125
Cefu Yuangui (冊府元龜) 60, 96
Chaek-sheng 124, 125
Cham gonu board 109, 111~113, 159
Chaoyang (朝陽) 51, 164, 231
Chen Wan's tombstone 202, 203
Chengshanzishan 81
Cheolli Malgal 55, 96, 97
Cheolli-bu 57, 82, 95, 151, 211
Cheonmun Pass (天門嶺) 148
Cheonson (天孫, Grandson of Heaven) 59, 132
Choi Chiwon (崔致遠) 23, 24, 39
Chukguk (蹴鞠) 156
Commemorative Special Stamp Set Dedicated to Dae Joyeong 31
Complete Works of Li Taibai (李太白全集) 171
composite ceiling 25
Concept of the "Southern and Northern Kingdoms" 24
Conquest of Korea (征韓論) 73, 74
Cotton from Okju 124
Cui Xin (崔忻) 38, 40, 41, 52, 94, 232, 233

Dae Balhae (大渤海) 210, 211, 215, 235
Dae Balhaeguk 209, 210
Dae Dorihaeng (大都利行) 60, 68, 71
Dae Gwanghyeon (大光顯) 200, 212, 214, 235
Dae Hyeonseok 103, 105, 237
Dae Inseon (大諲譔) 157, 188, 191, 199, 205, 206, 211, 234, 237

Dae Joyeong (the historical drama aired on KBS) 31
Dae Joyeong 22, 31~41, 48, 51, 55, 62, 81, 86, 93, 94, 96, 144, 147, 148, 152, 208, 209, 228, 231, 232, 237
Dae Munye (大門藝) 54, 68, 71, 152
Dae Woneui (大元義) 88, 99, 100, 237
Dae Yeollim 208, 209
Daeachan (大阿湌) 229
Daedong River 56, 71, 72
Daeheung (大興, Great Rising) 57, 60, 61, 85, 88, 145
Daemokdan mountain fortress 85
Daijoukan-cheop 137
Dajoukan (太政官, Great Council) 130
Danryeong (團領, a type of official robe) 162
Deer from Buyeo-bu 124
Dengzhou 65, 67~70, 119, 120, 152, 153
Deposed King (Dae Woneui) 99, 237
Diaspora 30, 36, 217, 231, 234~236
Diaspora in Korean history 231
divided minds 194, 195
Donggyeong (Baliancheng) 84
Donggyeong (東京, Eastern Capital) 56, 81, 86~88, 95, 117, 118, 180, 210, 211, 229
Dongpyeong-bu 56, 82, 95, 126
Dongyi (東夷) 42, 43
Double-bun hairstyle (雙髻) 165, 166
Dreaming of Balhae 31
Duke of Jinguo (震國公) 51
Duke of Xuguo (許國公) 51
Dunhua (敦化) 35, 81~83, 140, 150, 179

East Sea (東海) 33, 82, 116~118, 124, 193, 200, 229
Elementary Learning (小學諺解) 109
elevated style (高床式) 178
emissary to the Tang dynasty (遣唐使) 70
Emperor Hailing (海陵王) 219, 220, 224
Empress Hyoeui 61
Empress Sunmok 61, 63
Engi (延熹) era 171
Envoy ceremony (禮賓圖) 161

Eodae (魚袋) 162
Epitaph of the queen of King Mun (Empress Hyoeui) 61

Fanzhen (藩鎮, provincial military garrisons) 87
Five Dynasties period at the end of the Tang dynasty (唐末五代) 45
Fortress for Dae Inseon (大諲譔城) 234
Fujiwara Yoshitsugu (藤原良積) 176

Gaesim Buddhist Temple (開心寺) 170
Gaoli tujing (高麗圖經, Records of Goryeo) 184
Geolgeoljungsang (乞乞仲象) 51
Geolsabiu (乞四比羽) 51, 94
Go Gyeongsu (高景秀) 175
Go Yeongchang 210, 211
Goduri (高頭履) 166
Goguryeo (高句麗) 174, 178, 179, 182, 183, 185, 204, 207, 211, 212, 218, 219, 228, 231~233, 236
Goguryeo diaspora 231
Goguryeo revival movement 41, 192, 206, 210, 211
Gojoseon 42~44
Gonjil gonu 108
Gonu 230, 106~113, 157~159
Gonu board 109, 111~113, 158, 159
Gonu game 106, 107, 109, 110, 113, 157, 230
Gonu pieces 112, 158
Gonu road 110, 111, 113, 158, 230
Good horses 125, 127, 153, 156
Goryeosa (高麗史, History of Goryeo) 23, 189, 208, 210, 212, 235
Goryeosageolyo (高麗史節要, Essentials from the History of Goryeo) 212
Great Queen (太妃) 61
Guguk (舊國) 81, 84
Gujin qiguan (古今奇觀) 172
Guk-in (國人, central aristocrats) 88
Gulli 54

Gunseol 54
Gwadae (銙帶) 162
Gyeokgu (擊毬) 148~150, 156

Haedong (海東) 42, 43, 46
Haedongcheong (海東青) 127, 156, 165
Haedongseongguk (海東盛國, Flourishing Kingdom of the East) 17, 18, 32, 50, 55, 57, 64, 90, 99, 100, 103, 105, 116, 133, 154, 169, 171, 198, 205, 211, 228, 231, 235
Haeran fortress 84
Han chaocai (韓朝彩) 117
Hanamdun fortress 84
Hanamdun tomb complex 84
Hemp from Hyeonju 124
Heuksu 54, 101
Heuksu Malgal (黑水靺鞨) 53~55, 67, 68, 82, 93~97, 101, 118, 119, 131, 148, 151
Heungryoguk (興遼國) 208, 209, 211, 235
Hiroshi Machida (町田洋) 192
History of Balhae 14~19, 26, 30, 79, 103, 213, 216
History of the Southern and Northern Kingdoms 113, 116
Hoewon-bu 57, 82, 95
Hol (忽) 162
Hongjuneojang tomb complex 85
Honglujing stone monument (鴻臚井碑) 232
Horse of Solbin 124, 150, 156
Hosil 54
Huangtou Shiwei (黃頭室韋) 200
Hwa (靴) 162
Hyeokdae (革帶, leather belt) 162
Hyeondeok-bu in Junggyeong 126
Hyeonju (顯州) 124, 126, 167

Im Ah (任雅) 54
Imperial State 59, 63, 64, 86, 146
Inan (仁安, Benevolent Peace) 119
Incident at the Manbu Bridge (萬夫橋) 23, 26, 214, 235
Inscription of the Shrine Dedicated to Qian Liu, the King of the Wuyue Kingdom (吳越王錢公生祠堂碑) 45
Institution of the Crown Prince 64
Iron from the Wi-sheng 124

Jaemulbo (才物譜) 109
Jang Haengwon (張行愿)'s tombstone 217
Jang Ho (張造) 218~226
Jang Munhyu (張文休) 68, 151, 152
Jang Yeoyu (張汝猷)'s tombstone 217, 224
Japan 14, 16, 24, 30, 33, 54~56, 59, 62, 66, 68, 73~78, 93, 95, 98, 102, 103, 105, 116, 118, 121, 123, 127~137, 156, 167~169, 172, 175, 190, 192, 193, 205, 229, 232, 235
Japan Road 229
Japanese prince Shigeakira (重明親王) 168
Jeonganguk (定安國) 206, 207, 211, 215, 235
Jeongni-bu 56, 200
Jimi (羈縻, loose reign) policy 53
Jin (金) 176
Jinguk (震國) 33, 37, 39, 40, 41, 43~48, 51, 94, 120, 161, 231
Jin-neung 63
Jinshi (金史, History of the Jin) 218
Jiu Tangshu (舊唐書, Old Book of Tang) 21, 22, 37, 39, 53, 61, 92, 96, 169, 183, 233
Jiu Wudaishi (舊五代史) 45, 61
Jogosayin (詔誥舍人) 170
Joseon 15, 23, 27, 42~44, 4863, 73, 94, 97, 106, 109, 147, 156, 174, 183, 238
Ju Wonbaek (周元伯) 175
Jujagam (冑子監) 169
Jumong 25, 59, 218
Jungdaeseong (中臺省, Central Office) 130, 170
Jungdaeseong-cheop 136, 137
Junggyeong (中京, Central Capital) 56, 57, 69, 81~84, 95, 126, 150

Kaiyuan Era of Prosperity (開元之治, Kaiyuan Era of Prosperity) 74, 204
Ketugan(可突干) 68, 69, 71
Khitans (契丹) 16, 26, 65, 67~71, 77, 112, 151, 152, 157, 158, 164, 167, 188, 189~192, 195, 196, 199~211, 213~216, 218, 228, 231, 234
Kim Hongdo 106
King Dongmyeong (Jumong) 25, 218
King Gan (Dae Myeongchung) 100
King Gang (Dae Sunglin) 99, 100, 237
King Go (Dae Joyeong) 34, 144, 237
King Go of Balhae 30, 33~35, 55, 119, 120, 144, 229, 231, 237
King Gwanggaeto 25, 50, 59, 62
King Gyeongdeok 74~76
King Heui (Dae Eoneui) 100, 237
King Hyoso 229, 117
King Jeong (Dae Wonyu) 99, 100, 237
King Mu (Dae Muye) 18, 104, 144, 237
King Mun 18, 55, 57~64, 71, 72, 84~88, 95, 99, 100, 103, 132, 140, 142, 144, 160, 161, 170, 174, 234
King Mun, the Hwangsang 144
King of Jinguk (振國王, 震國王) 37, 41
King Seon (Dae Insu) 63, 99, 100, 237
King Seong (Dae Hwayeo) 88, 99, 100, 237
King Wang Geon (太祖 王建, the founder of Goryeo) 160, 213, 214, 216
King Yi Seonggye (太祖 李成桂, the founder of Joseon) 42
Kōdancho (江談抄) 171
Koksharovka Site, Yeonhaeju 166, 167
Korean diaspora 36
Kraskino, Yeonhaeju 110~112, 159~159, 229, 230

Later Balhae (後渤海) 205, 206, 215, 235
Later Liang dynasty (後梁) 45
Lee Heungseong (李興晟) 175
Lee Jinmong (已珍蒙) 172
Li Jinzhong 51

Liaodong Xinbuzhi (遼東行部志) 191
Liaoshi (遼史, History of Liao) 101, 188, 189, 194, 210, 234
Liaoyang (遼陽) 56, 200, 201, 202, 206, 210, 211, 218, 221
Line gonu 107, 108, 110
Lushun (旅順) 69, 151, 232

Maengbunwi (猛賁衛, Fierce Guard) 148
Makhil-bu 56, 95, 125, 200
Makyeogae 54
Malaek (抹額, red hemp headgear) 162
Malgal (靺鞨) 22, 25, 37~41, 48, 51~55, 57, 58, 65, 67~70, 72, 86, 92~98, 101, 118, 119, 124, 131, 148, 151, 161, 163, 164, 182, 212, 232, 233
Manwoldae in Gaeseong 112
Maritime and continental state (海陸國家, maritime and continental power) 33, 121
Memorial to Thank [the Tang emperor] for Not Allowing the Northern State (i.e., Balhae Envoys) to Sit Higher than [Silla Envoys] (謝不許北國居上表) 23, 34, 39
Miyako Kotomichi (都言道) 175
Mt. Dongmo (東牟山) 33, 35, 51, 52, 81, 83, 94, 231, 232
Mt. Liuding tomb complex 83, 140, 141, 146
Mt. Madou (馬都山) 69, 70, 121, 152, 153
Mt. Yongdu tomb complex 84
Munjeokwon (文籍院) 169

Namgyeong (南京, Southern Capital) 56, 82, 95, 117, 118, 125, 167
Namhae-bu (南海府, South Sea province) 82, 118, 167, 200, 206
Nestorian Christianity (景教) 121
Nihon shoki (日本書紀) 74
No sang 196, 205
Noble Queen (貴妃) 61
Noksa (錄事) 170

Northeast Project (東北工程) 16, 20, 39
Northeastern Jurchen (東北女直) 200
Novogoreevskoye 121

O Hyeonmyeong 207
Official documents (書契) 169
Okju (沃州) 124, 167
Ondol 25, 177, 181~185
Ondol culture 185

Pear from Nakyu 125
Pig of Makhil 125
Plan to Subjugate Silla 73
Plum from Hwando 125
prince Li Xian (李賢) 161
Princess Jeonghye's tomb 25, 146
Princess Jeonghyo 59, 61, 84, 142, 174
Princess Jeonghyo's tomb 142, 146, 162, 165
produce poems in seven steps (七步之才) 176
Pumpkin gonu 107, 110

Qian Liu (錢鏐) 45, 46
Qidan Guozhi (契丹國志, Records of the Khitan state) 56
Qidan Road 121
Queen Cheonchu (千秋太后) 213, 215
Queen of King Gan (Empress Sunmok) 61

Rabbits of the Mt. Taebaek 124
restirctions on Binggi (聘期, the interval between visits) 132
Ri (履) 162
Rice from No-sheng 125
Royal Tomb Institution 63
Ruiju kokushi (類聚國史) 102
Ruins of Yong-sheng 81

Sable Fur 124
Samguk sagi (三國史記, History of the Three Kingdoms) 21, 23, 56, 117, 229
Samguk yusa (三國遺事, Memories of the Three Kingdoms) 23
Samhan (三韓, Three Hans) 43, 44, 46, 48
Samo
Samryeongdun tomb complex 85
Sanggyeong (上京, Upper Capital) 16, 56, 57, 60, 81, 83~90, 95, 126, 150, 167, 180, 181, 196, 200, 205, 206, 229, 234
Sanggyeong Yongcheon-bu (上京 龍泉府) 16, 82, 167, 206
Sanggyeongseong (上京城) 33
Schism (釁) 188, 194, 195
scribes (書記) 22, 99, 117
Sea kelp 124, 125
Seal of Cheonmun Army (天門軍之印) 148
Seok Injeong (釋仁貞) 175
Seven-branched knife 62
Shawl (雲肩) 165
Shiwei (室韋) 121, 161, 200
Shoku Nihongi (續日本紀) 55, 59, 96, 149
Silk from Yongju 124
Silla (新羅) 16, 17, 23, 24, 26, 39, 42, 47, 52, 55~57, 62, 64, 66~69, 71~78, 82, 90, 94, 95, 100, 101, 112, 113, 116~119, 121, 131, 132, 135, 147, 152, 154, 156, 158~161, 169, 172, 174, 190, 205, 214, 229, 238
Silla Road (新羅道) 112, 117, 118, 121, 229
Silla Road of the South Sea 118
Silla translator (新羅學語) 172
Sillagwan (新羅館, Silla Office) 119
Silver chests 25
Site of the Aodong fortress 81
Small Fortress for Balhae (渤海小城)234
Sogdiana 87, 121
Solbin-bu 56, 82, 95, 125
Son Wanying 51
Songmal Malgal (粟末靺鞨) 22, 40, 93
Songmal Malgal people 25

Songmo jiwen (松漠紀聞) 147
Soswae Garden (濾灑園) 109
Southern and Northern Kingdoms (南北國) 16, 17, 24, 26, 27, 31, 64, 113, 116~118, 229, 230
Southern and Northern Kingdoms period 27
Soybean malt from the Chaek-sheng 124
Stele inscription of King Gwanggaeto (廣開土大王碑文) 25
Sui Tang yanyi (隋唐演義) 172
Suryeong (首領) 92, 93, 96, 97

Tagu (打毬) 149
Tang dynasty (唐) 21, 33, 35, 39~43, 45, 47, 51~53, 55, 65~71, 74, 75, 85~87, 93~96, 102, 103, 119, 120, 127, 128, 131, 148, 151, 164, 169, 171, 175, 176, 204, 231, 233
Tangbeiting (唐碑亭) 232
Theory of internal strife in Balhae 189
Tomb of the Dongjing (東京陵, Eastern Capital of Liao) 221
Tomb with a stone chamber with horizontal shafts 140, 145
Tuanjie in Dongning 182
Turkic characters 121
Turks (突厥) 24, 52, 53, 55, 65~68, 70, 94, 120, 128, 166, 205

Uighur (回紇) 87, 121, 157
Uighurs 121, 157
Ungwi (熊衛, Bear Guard) 148
Uru 54
Uru Malgal 96
Ussuriysk 156

various northern tribe (海北諸部) 65, 90
volcanic eruption of Mt. Baekdu 191~193, 198

Wang Hyoryeong (王孝廉) 175

Wang Mungu (王文矩) 149, 156
Wangseongguk (王城國) 76
Watching Gyeokgu in Early Spring (早春觀打毬) 149
Well gonu 107~110
Wen Tingyun (溫庭筠) 176
Wolheui 54, 57, 95, 101
Wolheui Malgal 55, 95~97, 148
Wu Chengci (烏承玼) 70, 152
Wugu (烏古) 200

Xara-balgas 113, 159
Xigucheng 84
Xin Tangshu (新唐書) 21, 22, 38, 39, 57, 61, 83, 92, 95, 99, 102~104, 117, 118, 125, 150~152, 162, 167, 169, 233
Xin Wudaishi (新五代史) 45
Xu Guidao (徐歸道) 75

Yang Seonggyu (楊成規) 175
Yao (遼) 176, 202, 203
Yelu Abaoji 56, 195, 199~204, 228, 234
Yelu Yaogu 202, 203
Yeol Manhwa 206, 207
Yeomju Fortress of Balhae 157
Yingzhou (營州) 51, 67, 69, 93, 94, 124, 152, 160, 204, 209, 231, 232
Yingzhou Road 121, 229
Yodong (遼東) 42, 51
Yongju (龍州) 124, 1126, 167
Yongwon-bu in Donggyeong 180
Yu Deukgong (柳得恭) 15, 23, 26, 156, 229
Yuchen Congtan (玉塵叢談) 171
Yuewu (越兀) 200

Zhendong (鎭東) 200, 201
Zizhi tongjian (資治通鑑, Comprehensive Mirror to Aid in Government) 56

Balhae,
The "Flourishing Kingdom of the East"
As The Successor to Goguryeo

Published on	November 30, 2023
Written by	Kim Eunkuk , Kwen Eunju, Kim Jinkwang
Publisher	Young-ho Lee
Published by	Northeast Asian History Foundation
Address	81, Tongil-ro, Seodaemun-gu, Seoul, Republic of Korea
Tel	02-2012-6065
Website	www.nahf.or.kr
Printed in	Nikebooks
ISBN	979-11-7161-014-3　03910

All rights reserved. No part of this publication may be used in any way that infringes copyright without prior written permission. To obtain copyright permission, please send a written inquiry to book@nahf.or.kr.